Model 4 Business

The Entrepreneur's Guide to

Clarity
Confidence
Credibility
Celebrity

Stephana Johnson

Model 4 Business The Entrepreneur's Guide to Clarity, Confidence, Credibility and Celebrity

Second Edition Copyright ©2021 by Stephana Johnson.
Book and Cover design by Kluba Creative
Cover photograph copyright Stephana

All rights reserved.
Printed in the United States of America. No part of this book may be used or reproduced or transmitted in any form or by any means without written permission from the author except in brief quotations embodied in critical articles or reviews.

Limited of Liability/Disclaimer of Warranty: While the publisher and author have used their best efforts in preparing this book, they make no representations or warranties with respect to the accuracy or completeness of the contents of this book and specifically disclaim any implied warranties or merchantability or fitness for a particular purpose. No warranty may be created or extended by sales representatives or written sales materials. The advice and strategies contained herein may not be suitable for your situation. You should consult with a professional where appropriate. The author shall not be liable for any loss of profit or any other commercial damage, including but not limited to special, incidental, consequential or other damages.

ISBN: 9781690822189

Independently Published.

DEDICATION

To my mom, Sara Oetinger; I am blessed that she taught and modeled for me a life of personal integrity, dedication to service and how to be a strong, independent woman.

To my Grandmothers, Muriel Evelyn Oetinger and Eva Paul Shank; I thank them for sharing with me their wisdom of healing, lineage of charity and strong independent spirit. Without their unconditional love and support, I would have a noticeable void in my life.

To entrepreneurs everywhere; never compromise your values and never give up on your dreams.

CONTENTS

INTRODUCTION

PART 1 - From Chaos To Clarity

PART 2 - From Doubt To Confidence

PART 3 - From Faking It To Credibility

PART 4 - From Unknown To Celebrity

THE PRACTICE - From Student To Mastery

About The Author

Acknowledgments

INTRODUCTION

Since my first profitable business at nine years old, I have reinvented myself and businesses for decades. Some were raving successes, others, epic failures.

When asked about my business model, I'd laugh and sometimes say, "to make it go right" ; which was my mom's business model, and I'm pretty sure her motto too. But "winging it" isn't a business model. It adds unnecessary steps, wastes time, energy, and money you may not have to spare.

In reading this book, as an entrepreneur, you may find yourself closer to the pre-levels of the C4 Mastery. Realize it's not a bad thing and doesn't define you. Take it as information that can be very useful in helping you shift to your next higher level.

And be glad this book is in your hands! It walks you through the C4 of my Model 4 Business (puns intended). When you have complete mastery of your Clarity, Confidence, Credibility and Celebrity, you will be self-igniting Dynamite!

Stephana Johnson   www.model4business.com

CHAOS TO CLARITY

SETTING THE STAGE

Buzzing with vibrant energy, as the 15 year old "star" of the Givenchy show, I weightlessly walk the catwalk in Givenchy's beautiful butterfly finale dress. I was living my dream. With some of the wealthiest and most influential people in the audience, captivated by what I effortlessly exuded; I was using my own unique form of C4: graceful clarity, calm confidence, natural credibility, and innate celebrity.

Since I can remember, I wanted to be center stage, making people feel as if there was something magical to be discovered. I would take on different personas to effect positive change. I was awed by the gift of completely living truthfully in some imaginary circumstance and the powerful impact it could have to shift another's reality toward something more positive. I watched and learned how this would happen in Betty Davis films, with Rita Hayworth and later Diane Keaton.
My favorites.

By the time I was 11, I caught the modeling bug. I skipped the teen magazines and instead subscribed to Glamour, Vogue, Elle; copying every make up, hair style and fashion look throughout those pages.

Waking long before sunrise; showering, shaving, scrubbing, plucking, washing, blowing, curling, then applying full make up and wardrobe, head to toe accessorized, I was nothing short of obsessed. I wouldn't leave the house without this full ritual completed.

Becoming proficient, I could emulate any style of hair or makeup I'd seen. And I was an eclectic fashionista.

By the time I was 12, I was begging my parents for modeling school. While I already had my own $35 a week salary, cleaning a beauty salon; a job I inherited from my moms successful cleaning business, it wasn't going to cut the $1200 modeling training. But my parents made it go right, even though we had little money to spare..

Not long after, I signed with a top agent in Scottsdale and booked my first gig. It was a maternity mannequin modeling job. That's where a live person dresses in the stores clothing, in my case maternity wear, then stands perfectly still for 15 minutes on a platform in the middle of the mall.

I could be that perfect, unblinking statue - effortlessly. It was fabulous! The more the shoppers stopped to gape, their "oohs and aahs" and questions of was I flesh and blood or not, spurred my determination to be the best at my job.

KNOWING VS UNDERSTANDING

Before I got my drivers license, my mom would juggle her work to get me to my auditions and bookings. My brothers and I still helped in her cleaning business every Tuesday and Sunday, and I still cleaned the beauty salon. I also doubled down on my high school to graduate 2 1/2 years early, knowing clearly I wanted to head to New York City as soon as possible.

Between 14 and 16, I was regularly appearing in the paper and local magazines, landing on several covers. I was being booked for bit parts in films and commercials and even being recognized on the street.

I recall the first time someone came up asking for my autograph. I had been speaking to a high school assembly, hired as a celebrity spokesperson for the "Say No To Drugs Campaign" . A young man (keep in mind I was barely out of high school myself) came up to me with a magazine opened to a page, asking if I'd sign the photo.

 At first, I really had no idea what he was talking about. But then he showed me the photo. How exciting! It most certainly was me in a beautiful blue outfit from a shoot I enjoyed very much.

My enthusiastic appreciation of his appreciation made us both laugh, and he commented on how "real" I was in person.

However, I rarely knew exactly when or what photos the photographer or magazine would end up using. I had stopped keeping track of when my work came out. Instead, I began focusing on the next job and the next.

But having this kind young man honoring me with his request, I was humbled and excited at the same time. He shared a gift with me that day.

We must celebrate, even the small wins, as we progress toward our dreams and goals. If we do not, they will diminish and we might miss when we've fulfilled our youthful dreams and when it's time to make bigger ones.

CONFUSED ILLUSIONS

Sitting with a couple of beautiful models, preparing our makeup for the swim-wear fashion show, we chatted about an up coming wedding in the Hampton's, when top model of the '80's, Christie Brinkley walked by. We had heard there was a celebrity as the featured model, we guessed that it must be her. But she looked unwell, with terrible acne and nearly unrecognizable without her "face" on.

It was not what I had come to expect from "celebrity". The girls and I went about our chatting, noting just what amazing make-up can do for someone. But I felt confused, betrayed even. Because the woman I saw that day, was not the stunning woman on the cover of Sports Illustrated or all the magazines of my childhood that I aspired to be.

COPYCATS LOSE CREDIBILITY

I was antsy as I sat across from my agent at the Wilhelmina Modeling Agency, discussing the contract to go to Barcelona for swim-wear season. I just couldn't make a decision. Feeling confused and uncertain about something that should have been so clear, I fretted for days.

Since moving to NYC, I was being booked regularly, but not for covers of Vogue or Glamour like I dreamed of. Instead, I was being booked for swim-wear, lingerie and catalogue work. Because I had always been in to health and fitness, thanks to my mom, instead of smoking and purging like many other models to stay stick thin, I didn't need to. I was either teaching aerobics at the gym, riding my bike or roller blading through the city, easily staying lean and strong. I also ate more health consciously rather than binging and purging I had observed some of my peers doing.

Not only was I not twiggy thin, I had a few curves and a C cup size on the top. It was only natural that I'd be booked for my body, working regularly for top swim-wear and lingerie companies.

However, I still tried to copy the latest stick thin runway and cover models instead of embracing what I was naturally gifted with. Not to mention that it was actually more profitable and enjoyable. But my yard stick had been set when I was much younger; against the cover models and stick thin, pale, unsmiling girls. So I had gotten stuck in the pattern of copying the magazines instead of embracing what was right there in front of me. My vibrant health and playful confidence had given me natural credibility and catapulted me to celebrity, without me even trying. Yet I refused to acknowledge this and continued to compare where I wasn't against where I thought I wanted to be.

COMPARE YOURSELF WITH YOUR OWN PROGRESS

Barcelona, Spain was calling me as the swim-wear season in NYC was coming to a close. My agent was excited and trying to convince me that this was the best thing to do right now. Our sister agency in Spain, would take care of all the accommodations and flight; my day rate was a whopping 10K and this was in the 1980's.

I could easily work for a month or 6 weeks and come home with a fat bank account. What was I even thinking twice about? That night I sat down with my fiance I'd been living with for the last couple of months and shared my excitement and the plan. His response was, "how do you know I'll still be here when you get back"?

That was his way of letting me know the ultimatum. Barcelona or him. I chose him over my career, that day, but the relationship ended less than year later anyway.

Over the years, I would still compare and define myself by those who seemed to be where I thought I wanted to be. Had I stopped to evaluate my progress early on, deciphering what was working and what wasn't, I could've reinforced what was effective and eliminated what was useless. But sometimes experience is a dear teacher we must endure ourselves.

However, I hope in sharing some of my personal stories, it will illustrate lessons you don't have to experience first hand.

USE A SOLID FRAME OF REFERENCE

When I first moved to NYC in 1986, my mom helped me get set up in an apartment in a suburb of Brooklyn, NY. I found a little weekend job as a medical assistant to help pay rent while I auditioned during the week. I basically handled the urine samples, greeted patients and took care of their paper work.

The doctor and his patients were an eclectic mix of colorful, wonderful characters. I loved it! I would put on my white lab coat, an acting prop I had in my trunk of costumes, and literally dress the part.

My enthusiasm and passion was contagious. I genuinely cared about each person I met, and was interested in them and their lives. It was fun for me to play that role. On the subway rides into NYC for auditions, I would study psychology and self help books, seeking answers to questions burning inside. At night, I'd come back and teach aerobics classes at the local little gym. A busy beaver with abundant energy.

Although my confidence was high in some areas, it was from a foundation that I no longer had in place, now that I was living on my own in the big city.

I was speedily moving through my life, building it based on my youthful passions and ideas of what I imagined I should be doing. I thought I was clear on my purpose: to be a successful working actress and model.

Success to me at that time, meant winning an Academy Award and being on the cover of Vogue. A pretty high bar I had set, but I was clear none the less.

Health and fitness was intrinsic to who I was at my core, having grown up surrounded by it. That was a natural side gig. Plus getting paid to stay fit was a nice benefit.

But as I had more and more balls to juggle, my once very graceful clarity started to become clouded and expressed itself in my dwindling confidence.

This is a very dangerous state, because others prey on this type of energy. What's more, when you find yourself in this type of energy, you might attract others outside yourself that are not in alignment with your own inner C4.

Although I had certainty in my career goals and the energy to achieve them, I didn't have an understanding of how my goals would balance with the rest of my life.

I wanted a relationship, but I neglected to evaluate what kind of relationship. Forgoing the trip to Barcelona to avoid losing a relationship that turned out to be superficial anyway, was a tough lesson. But it brings to focus another key concept I want to teach you here:

We have to **determine, for ourselves, our own life purpose and priorities, so we can align our actions.**

When faced with a choice that is clearly not in harmony with your purpose, your answer should be an easy one. I help my clients discover their own life purpose, as well as align it to a specific framework. In this book, I will provide a given framework for you to use, as you work toward your C4 Mastery.

The framework is built on 4 pillars: **Energy, Work, Love and Wisdom. Energy** is what propels us to carry out our purpose. This includes proper sleep, movement, nutrition, water and other health maintaining actions. **Work** is what you are here to do, your unique contribution, your life purpose. **Love**, including self love, romantic love, family and friends as well as community, brings belonging, connection, appreciation and is often the elixir that motivates us even higher. **Wisdom** brings us understanding, insight, truth and freedom; it is often the synthesizer that helps us level up in continuous progress and to what I call your C4 Mastery.

Each intertwined and intricately connected to bring about a harmonious and optimally functioning and prosperous individual and organization.

They are constantly in play with one another and keeping these in harmony, by practicing daily habits I will share, you will have a powerful framework for a meaningful business and life, as you move from student to mastery, more proactively.

As I mentioned above, when I chose my relationship

over going to Barcelona, I had certainty, but not clarity. I was certain I wanted to be married, but I did not have the clarity on who that person would be, how we would be together or if they would be supportive of my chosen career. As a result, I made a decision based on disharmony and thus a natural contraction, rather than expansion, of my career and life resulted.

Understanding this framework now, I am much better able to make decisions that have long term positive effects, resulting in continuous harmony and expansion aligned with my values.

We will begin to use this framework as a key component going forward on your path to C4 Mastery.

CLARITY TEACHING POINTS

Don't Be a Copy Cat. Do you.

You will experience the most rewards both intrinsically and externally when you come from a place of truth within yourself and your own goals and dreams.

Where you are now, is different than where you have been. Where someone else is, has nothing to do with you. What other people think of you, also, has nothing to do with you. The sooner you get clear on that, the sooner you'll shift out of the lower states of confusion.

No one can be all things to all people. Embrace the fact that you are unique, one of a kind, and YOU know YOU best! I want to help you remember that.

Clients seek me out because I do see them. I can clearly separate all the facade, copy catting, and "faking it", that they've put up about themselves, knowingly or unknowingly.

It's like Michelangelo said in carving David, "I saw the angel in the marble and carved until I set him free"¹"

I'm grateful to be a facilitator to your own discovery of You; supporting you as you chisel away all the excess that is not You, so you can live Your Masterpiece.

CLARITY QUEST

What are you the very best at?

What brings you the absolute most joy?

What is also the most profitable for you?

Within these three questions is where you will find your unique gift to share, your "˜secret sauce'.

This is also what those you are here to serve will most readily recognize as valuable. It is what makes you "the expert", gets you noticed and shared like candy.

This is what your market will unfold from. Don't make it more complicated than that. Don't get caught up in this game of trying to "find your niche". It's not lost, and it never has been. You've just been looking outside at everyone else, trying to see it through a lens that's clouded with the illusions of others you bought into.

It doesn't matter how someone else made it, we can't copy what they are doing and be successful. Don't imagine "˜if you just do what they did', or follow their steps, that you'll get the same results or even that you should. That's not how it works.

BONUS: You can download a supplemental workbook at www.model4business.com/workbook, a great resource to document your steps and progress as well as a few added surprises!

Stephana Johnson   www.model4business.com

CLARITY AFFIRM ACTIONS

1. Unsubscribe from all copy cat lists you're on, so you stop the comparison wheel. Turn off every feed and podcast that triggers competition in you. At least for the next 6 weeks. Decide to focus on your own C4 Mastery.

You must stop comparing yourself to others and stop copying what others are doing. Not only do you not know anything about their specific circumstances, nor their journey along the way, you have no clue how long they've been at it or what was the force that propelled them to their place. Your action steps, strategy and tactics are unique to you and where you are. It's ineffective to compare your beginning to another's end. It's also irrelevant to your success.

2. Delete this question from your thought patterns "Am I worthy?" Of course you are worthy! And while we're at it: Of course you are worth that much! *Note that every person's "worthiness" number is different. We'll address your pricing and packaging soon. But it should have NOTHING to do with your worthiness. So let's stop that confusion right now.

Your action step is to detach your worthiness from any number. We'll get into the whole "get paid what you are worth" dance later. For now, getting clear on this piece is crucial for your inner Clarity.

Stephana Johnson   www.model4business.com

SELF DOUBT TO CONFIDENCE

WHAT DOESN'T KILL YOU MAKES YOU STRONGER

My heart was racing and I was seeing fuzzy auras. I lay on my back staring down at my bare, 10 year old feet; one normal sized and one gigantic, to my mind, elephant sized. We had come out to northern Florida to visit Granny and Grandpa; Dad's parents who were mysterious and wise.

My dad had been working on the tractor off in the field, my younger brothers off on some adventure and I was raking leaves near the little cottage house in my flip flops.

I may have registered the pain of the stings, but was used to mosquitoes so brushed it off, working away diligently. By the time I realized I was horizontal, my dad began explaining I had stepped into a nest of baby water moccasins and had been bitten.

I was calm because my dad was calm. The venom coursed through my veins and by the time anyone was aware of what had happened, the venom was already in my system. My grandmother, a folk healer, had instructed my dad on how to handle it. He confidently took action, using an herb poultice on the bite area and serving me some bitter tea. I laid in bed for hours in and out of dreams, as my dad bolstered my confidence that all would be well. The poison was assimilated through my body over a period of time.

Neither grandparents made a big deal over the snake bite. While I could tell my dad was concerned, he remained pro-active, although taking no unnecessary actions. His calm confidence was more medicine than any anti- venom.

My grandmother was a tiny thing, skin and bones, and not quite 5 feet of ferociousness. With a high pitched, but gravely voice from having her jaw broken, throat crushed and rebuilt after a horrific auto accident, it only made her more cantankerous. What she lacked in height she made up with wisdom and determination.

I recall sitting with my granny, a rare event as I was a bit fearful of her. However, she shared her love of learning and books with me; one in particular was Think and Grow Rich by Napoleon Hill. This singular book would become my guiding force and to this day I recommend it to all as required study. I still keep her copy with me as a resource for common sense wisdom in an age of high priced snake oil and quick rich schemes.

My grandfather who was retired military having fought in WWII, was stoic but kind. They were intelligent, hard people. I understood and admired my father's calm confidence all the more after being around his parents.

EAT YOUR POISON

Did you know that the peacock eats poisonous plants to make his tail feathers more beautiful and brilliant?

When I first heard about this from Pema Chodron's teachings, I fell in love with this idea. My admiration for peacocks is great, and as an avid admirer of art, it is easy to forget the work and sometimes great sacrifice, that goes into creating such beauty.

In life, and in business, there will be circumstances and situations that are seemingly utterly insurmountable. I've had many myself, and have even tried to avoid the inevitable challenges. But if we embrace the idea of the peacock, we embrace the "poison" as something that will not only NOT kill us, but on the contrary, make for luminous tail feathers.

In evolving over the years in this way, I learned the process of transmuting obstacles into the path, challenges into strengths, poison into medicine.

With this perspective, it is much more meaningful when you look at the big picture, while also embracing the intricate nuances of being deep in the process.

As a recovering perfectionist, with very set outcomes of win or lose, this frame of mind has taken me some time to integrate. However, when you discover this subtle shift for yourself, I believe you will also find a more direct path to clarity, which will then bring an unshakable confidence for you.

Early in life, I believed that the challenge was something I must endure, thinking that if I could just get through it, grin and bear it, then I'd be safe and free on the other side.

Before that time, I looked at escaping, avoiding or forcing my way through, rather than embracing and learning from the challenges. This avoidance only lengthens the process and we often miss some of our best experiences.

Judging everything on a scale of black or white, good or bad, right or wrong, we miss our true potential.

If you believe that you must be in a certain condition or reach a certain state in order to be successful, you will consider anything short of that, unsuccessful. Thus you would be diminishing the potential gains of the journey itself.

If you believe that certain aspects of your character are unchangeable, that it's "just your nature" or fate, you will create in your mind a constant need to justify and prove yourself worthy in that.

In the past, I often identified myself with the circumstance or experience, identifying myself as the: failure, loser, winner, star, etc.

That rigid outlook to life can sabotage even the most strong and talented among us.

However, if you believe that your past, or your characteristics and innate qualities, are a point of potentiality, you begin to take on a different focus and expand as a result.

Understanding our past as something that is helpful rather than bad, shameful or to be hidden, we can uncover an expanded sense of comprehension and therefore a deeper sense of our inner C4 - clarity, confidence, credibility and celebrity, for ourselves.

Having rigid belief systems, we judge everything through that lens, thwarting our own ability to know for ourselves, what is truly possible. Often we have had help in building that fixed mindset, and just like identifying yourself as the condition, you cannot unravel it at the same point of creation. But once you become aware of the mechanism, you open up your world to possibilities in a whole new way.

That's my passion. That is the transformation I am here to help you unfold. While it can be a painful process, like the caterpillar becoming a butterfly, we have to trust the metamorphosis.

To trust that it is in our DNA to be fully who we are here to be. Clear that we have in ourselves, innately, the pure potential for its unfolding, and the steadfast confidence to express that through our life's work.

I have learned to be more gentle and patient, both with myself and the results. I have learned to focus on the process rather than the outcome and to take each step as information. Not as judgment but as an observation that I can use to propel myself forward, culminating in a much more fulfilling and rewarding experience of life.

So I will say this to you, when you feel utterly defeated and feel like the obstacles are insurmountable, don't give up! Be confident that your challenge is the doorway to your mastery.

CONFIDENCE BUILDING CREDIBILITY

It was the mid 90's and I was on the set of Armageddon, literally living my dream. I was dating a guy I loved, had a great apartment in Los Angeles, competent in my craft, strong in my body from my side business of fitness, and confidently taking step by step actions toward the success I was after.

I had joined a business coaching group called The Actors Network® and was starting to land jobs regularly. I had a system for auditioning that shifted my view of the no's I faced, and I stopped taking them personally.

I eliminated the busy work and focused on the action steps with a work flow set up that was effective.

These are the key metrics I used and tracked on a daily basis:

Send mail submission / electronic submission

Personal Letter Sent (to casting directors, directors, producers, et. al.)

10 pieces of general info sent (mass mailings like postcards promoting a show I was in or something I just completed)

Personal Contact for Showcase (required research and creating a data base)

Personal Contact social event

Call to a Casting Director/Rep

Call to Director

Personal Drop off (of head shot and resume)

Personal Drop off with a gift

Meeting or Interview

Lunches/Dinners with key Industry players

All I had to do was look over that sheet and I could see a correlation between my number of auditions and ultimately my revenue from acting, knowing just how to adjust things. The more I did of the above, the more auditions I went on. Auditions which led to bookings, which led to income, which led to security, which led to recognition, which led to more work - in a fairly predictable manner.

It was no longer luck. It took the "fake it 'til you make it" out of the equation. I was working smart, with clarity about what I needed to be doing and the confidence that I could get those actions done. I knew how to get the right help at the right time, improving in the essential areas to see tangible, increasing results.

There was no more mystery of "how come she got that

part and I didn't". In a business that's completely subjective, I took what I could under my control, and found a proactive way to do what I loved.

I also knew what **I shouldn't be doing**. There are always lots of things we shouldn't be doing, and those are usually the areas that trip us up the most. We have to learn to **differentiate between the essential few and the seemingly important many**.

I created a point system for my business actions that were tangible. For example, I tracked:

Of minutes rehearsing

Of auditions completed (I counted showing up, not just landing the gig!)

Of hours completed on set (this helped me re-frame 14 hour days on the set as a positive rather than negative!)

Of $ put toward my pension

Of words about me in the paper (didn't care if they were good or bad)

I also tracked my gross revenue and my net revenue, so I was clear on what my costs were in relationship to my income.

I set up a separate business identity, incorporating myself. So I was running a business, not being the business.

This also helped me step out of the energy of it being about me personally, because I was running a business with numbers I could track.

Subsequently, I wasn't spending time "˜down' because I didn't get a gig; a nasty perpetuating cycle that can be very dangerous in all areas of life and business.

Counting showing up as a win, prepared and professional, improved the most valuable asset I had, ME.

Being focused, present, calm and kind to everyone from the doorman to the director, was a win and left lasting impressions. It was the right actions I was rewarding, not the outcome.

By getting so clear on what the few essential actions really were: improving my craft in acting class, taking a specialized class for auditions or commercials, rehearsing; I fully embraced my business. And my confidence grew!

Auditioning had been my greatest challenge before, but when I shifted it to being an essential part of the overall process, not an end in and of itself, it had become fun again.

I even learned to take feedback, criticism and snarky comments, as a way to improve, rather than something to tear me down.

As I sat on the set in the oh so comfy, giant barker lounges lined up; they were needed because the costumes of space suits, were huge, I felt at peace. While my role was a very simple one, with a single line, I was home. I felt more than content, I felt I belonged. And it was bliss.

CONFIDENCE TEACHING POINTS

The number one reason for self doubt is the belief we should be something we are not.

When we refuse to appreciate and honor our own unique abilities, that is self-sabotage.

Don't run your life or business so fast that you not only forget where you've been, but you forget where you are going.

Nothing is a waste of time if you use the experience wisely.

Do not let anything that is not in alignment with your framework take up mental space in your brain.

Eliminate all non-essential actions.

Organize, track and make practical use of the facts in an orderly fashion. The right metrics and numbers will bring calm and confident choices.

CONFIDENCE QUESTS

Your self-image and your habits go together. Change one and you automatically change the other. Are you wearing clothes of a depressed, angry, confused person? Well, go change. Right now!

Ask yourself - what new choice can I make as a result of this new understanding?

What do I need to delete, release or DE-story from my life right now?

What do I need to reinforce, improve or tell a new story about in my life right now?

Write the actions out in your journal or in this book.

Choose 2 small actions you will take today, and go do them now.

CONFIDENCE AFFIRM ACTIONS

1. Impose certain restrictions on your thoughts. If you know you have self limiting thoughts that come up around you confidently stepping fully into the best version of you, impose specific restrictions on your thoughts.

Most people let their negative thoughts run their lives, right down into depression, self doubt and chaos. After working countless hours in cognitive therapy, I'm clear one doesn't need to go kicking around skeletons, you **can** CHOOSE. Choose to focus on happy, pleasing incidents and re-frame your past. It works, believe me.

2. RE-FRAME. In thinking of the past, present, or future, deliberately train your attention to a desirable element and learn to FOCUS. Build on this action. It will take practice and some time but the resultant self confidence will be noticeable.

--BONUS--

Don't forget to download the supplemental workbook at www. model4business. com/ workbook, so you can write down your thoughts all in one place.

FAKING IT TO CREDIBILITY

LEVELING IT OUT

I worked in, dated and later married a musician, so I've been in and around the music industry since the 80's working at Arista. While I can't sing a lick, I admire the heck out of real musicians.

One musician guy I dated had a professional studio in his home. He had produced some big name rock bands and I was privy to a lot of scoop, as well as some wild back stage shenanigans.

However, in the studio there is some serious business that goes on. I had already worked at Arista records and met Milli Vanilli. I had heard about the lip sync "scandal", but it didn't mean too much to me, for two reasons: I rarely if ever judged another as harshly as I judged myself, and I really didn't understand the big deal. These guys were adorable and actually very talented. But to a true artist, it's apparently pretty shameful.

So, when the producer I was dating took me into his studio and had me sing my favorite song, embarrassed to no end, he told me, "trust me, just sing the way you do in the shower and you think no one is listening." Oh dear. Most likely he heard my rendition of "Gypsy's

Tramps and Thieves" just that morning.

I sang what I knew by heart and had a little fun doing it. Then he had me sit next to him in front of this enormous mixing board. Playing with a few knobs and levels, he changed what honestly sounded like a sick cat, to something that sounded unique and interesting. It was fascinating what one could do with a bit of shifting with these levels and knobs.

While an excellent singer or musician can and does make beautiful music, the professional mixer can sharpen or distort, add resonance, reverb, echo, lower the bass, or reduce pitch; all to make a masterpiece.

Music making wasn't in my cards, but I really liked this concept of altering levels to create harmony.

When I speak about this to audiences, I can demonstrate it with the sound man, bringing clarity to mid tones and lessoning high pitch notes that don't resonate with the overall desired outcome.

We can use this idea in our own lives as well. In C4 Mastery, we are wanting to create harmonious levels across the board and that requires us to level up areas of clarity and confidence or credibility and celebrity.

However, we want to do this from an authentic place, so the resonance is balanced with our own internal highest set point. We never want to try to match someone else's pitch. It's been said before, be the best you, not a second rate version of someone else.

It's not that we can't learn from another, or experience greater understanding, but we need to come at this from our own, what I like to call, unique "soul's song".

I believe everyone has their own unique soul's song and when they are in harmony with that, that's when the magic happens. There is something very beautiful and genuine in that level of clarity and the output contributes to internal and external authentic credibility.

It can't be forced and it really can't be fabricated. You've noticed the difference in your own area of expertise, I'm sure. Let's take an artist like Whitney Houston or Michael Jackson, you just can't copy that. In fact, it just makes the person trying to copy, that much more like a fraud. Don't pretend to be someone you are not, that's the fastest way to lose credibility.

FAKE AMATEURS VS REAL PROS

I had really just lucked into the job at Arista Records. The musician I was dating, who had held the gig for a while, was going on a tour and asked if I'd fill in for him. What that meant is I would arrive at 6pm taking over for the day receptionist and hold the desk until midnight. I'd also be there from 9-6 on the weekends. Perfect, because most of my auditions and modeling or acting jobs were during the week days.

The 9th floor housed the founder and mega record producer, Clive Davis, where his office covered half the entire floor. The A&R department was also on this floor, so I would get to hear the countless demo tapes played.

After hearing the song stop at only a few seconds in, my ear became tuned to what was a hit and was considered not. Most of the NOTs were copy like material. But when something with a unique, genuine quality came on, the difference was unmistakable.

I was rarely phased by the level of celebrity that called to be put through to Mr. Davis, nor surprised by those who walked through the elevator doors. Whether it was the stunning Whitney Houston, sharp dressed Barry Manilow; a consummate gentleman usually surrounded by an arrogant entourage, or the scrappy Taylor Dayne, I was professional and kind.

There were quite a few perks to this job. I was privy to

people and their situations one rarely sees. Providing calm assistance or support as needed. I was immersed in the comings and goings, whether through the front or back doors and engaged with some of the most talented and well respected artists and entrepreneurs of our time.

Here's some of what I learned:

Celebrities who are doing the work as professional artists are genuinely good people. The amateurs tend to have a facade, and if you are in harmony with your own values and framework, then it's very easy to spot.

The professional is confident there is real work to be done and they get down to it, day in, day out. You won't find them resting on last weeks hit. They have developed daily habits and are disciplined in those mundane tasks, rarely letting demons distract them from the work at hand. That makes their gift look effortless to outsiders. All too often, the amateurs will shout "but it's so easy for them!"

They host no need to put others down in order to feel worthy. They tend to do the work without needing to focus on the recognition or the competition. They focus on the process first and don't obsess over the outcome. They do the work because they must; it's who they are. To do anything less would be to live a lie and suffer a slow, painful death.

It is usually the entourage that you have to worry about. Their trust issues are huge and they'll tear you to shreds, just to give you the time of day.

Often they are harboring dreams to be the star, seemingly protecting the celebrity while covertly sabotaging them. They act like they don't care, not about you, not about anything. They sometimes act like they own the place. Clive Davis, who **did** own the place, NEVER acted that way. He had a presence and a penetrating focus that was unmistakable power. I wanted that kind of impeccable dynamism. That's what I strive for in myself and for my clients, daily.

Mr. Davis had put in the time, he'd done the work. Day in, day out. He built his record company with a singularity of purpose, confident in his path and proving credible, as he scouted and developed some of the best artists we have come to know and celebrate today.

He did it with consistent, persistent, diligent focus and is still doing it today, at age 87. Indeed a powerful example of C4 Mastery.

CREDIBILITY TEACHING POINTS

To be credible is to be believed in, to be trustworthy.

You first must believe in yourself.

Can you look yourself in the mirror and trust that you are fully showing up and working toward the best version of you?

Everything you do is a practice. So, what are you practicing at? Each thought, each action is an opportunity to practice. Start with being the best version of you, in harmony with your framework. This is the best way to build genuine credibility, through this process.

CREDIBILITY QUESTS

Choose how you spend your days. Start the night before, checking the harmony levels of your C4 with your Energy, Work, Love, Wisdom. Do you know where you need to up level your results? Write down the one action you will reinforce and one action you will release.

Where do you need to stop 'faking it' and instead, create well defined, measurable action steps, that will take you to real credibility?

Are you being effective in your actions? Far too many entrepreneurs are overworked but unproductive. Their actions are not aligned with a singular point of focus.

Remember, your goal is the singular point of focus at this time. Think about the top of one specific mountain. You can only ever be climbing one mountain at a time.

Do you need to reevaluate if it is the mountain you want to summit? If yes, then get crystal clear on YOUR goal right now. That's a clarity point. Once you have that singular point of focus, it's much easier to get your thoughts, actions and daily habits, aligned.

To build that credibility takes daily, consistent, specific step by step actions. Staying with that mountain analogy a bit longer, what is required for you to make it safely up the mountain?

Do you know what provisions you need?

Are you prepared for and with the correct provisions?

At the end of your work day, take a fresh look at what you are aiming for, evaluate your process and progress.

Reset your sites so they are even more precise. Then go to sleep with that clarity so your body and mind can rest and recharge.

Get up and get after it with that singular point of focus.

This is how you will build momentum.

Singularity of purpose is a powerful point of credibility. What do you need to jettison to make things even more streamlined toward your goal?

What needs to be repaired, restored, refueled?

CREDIBILITY AFFIRM ACTIONS

You are not your mistakes, but you need to learn from your mistakes. You will build credibility by admitting them (to yourself) not as blame, but as a point of understanding, so you can grow.

Accept yourself.

Be yourself.

Trust that you can know.

But be willing to let go of the countless distractions, so that you can go with what your deepest calling has in store for you.

Then go forward with that clarity and confidence, with consistent, ever increasing competency. That's how you build compounding credibility.

--BONUS--

Be sure to download the supplemental workbook at www. model4business. com/ workbook, a great resource to document your steps and progress.

FROM UNKNOWN TO CELEBRITY

You now know what makes you stand out and you have the confidence to bring that to center stage for your life and business. Getting clear on what you want to be known for, to yourself as well as others, needs to be in harmony with your framework.

We are now going to focus on making you and your expertise, well known and well thought of.

One rarely becomes a celebrity without the help of other people, without recognition and attention. This isn't the time to hide out. It doesn't mean you have to go on every talk show out there, but it does mean you need to be willing to be seen and heard, or at least your business does.

Part of being recognized and celebrated has a lot to do with how you show up. Be clear on what you want to be known and remembered for. I'm sure you can think of a few "celebrities" you wouldn't want to be known as.

We are also not looking for the 15 minutes of fame. We want you and your business to be noticed and shared because you provide a unique and valuable solution to a problem people want solved.

PAYING THE DUES

Late into the night, I was putting the finishing touches on the red wall, tightening brackets to the ballet bar and celebrating how far I'd come. My dream studio was a reality, with beautiful floating wood floors and floor to ceiling mirrored walls.

Differentiated clearly from all the other yoga studios, box gyms and trainers out there, Yogilachi® is the perfect blend of yoga, Pilates and tai chi.

We help our clients get toned and free of pain, without pills or surgery. Providing a boutique style, judgment free and family like community, we attract our ideal clients effortlessly.

Because we were completely clear on who we were, how we were unique and valuable with specific outcomes attained for each of our clients, we were able to charge premium prices and attract the right kind of clients consistently from the very beginning.

We didn't accept everyone into the studio, nor did we want just anyone. Not because we were being snooty, but because we knew who we were and who we serve. We were confident saying NO when they weren't the right fit, because we knew that the right client would find us. And they did, to a wait list.

Colleagues appreciated us because we weren't their

competition or trying to steal their clients. Instead, we were fellow collaborators, with a mission to help improve the health and fitness of our community in our specialized way.

Those that were repelled by our message and methods were not our people. We were more than OK with this. Our reviews and testimonials spoke volumes and came in on their own.

We'd celebrate our clients and created systems to honor our members. Consistently delivering excellent results, with a beautiful space, a great location, and well designed marketing and signage, we quickly became the leading brand in our market.

We would surprise our clients with flowers delivered to them at their offices on their birthday. We would support them when there was a family emergency. We cared that much. We loved what we were doing and it showed!

Our ideal market naturally wanted to be a part of that, to work with us and for us!

The Yogilachi brand had been ignited and is a prime example of C4 Mastery. By using this Model 4 Business, it was faster and far simpler, as well as exponentially more rewarding than we'd been led to believe before.

In closing this section, I want to share with you about a

different type of celebrity and dues paying, that I disagree with.

I had invited one of the top sitcom stars of the 90s and her husband over for a home cooked meal. I had known her from acting class and we were in similar social circles. We weren't besties and at this stage her husband had now become a bit protective of her. She herself was unassuming and full of joy, as she sat on the floor of my kitchen, playing with my new kitten.

She hadn't changed, in spite of the $2 million an episode paychecks.

As we sat around the table talking, the husband, with a thick facade, and her, just being herself; giving, open, and humble, I asked her what it was that had catapulted her to success.

She described being herself, showing up fully with a singular point of focus. But her husband asserted the reason she'd become a celebrity was because they had paid tithe to the church. She didn't agree or disagree.

Observing the two, I saw one making things convoluted and complicated, and thus struggling themselves, and the other, embodying what I came to create and distill into my signature program C4 Mastery.

The simplicity of your own C4 Mastery can't be underestimated. Things get made to seem more complex and esoteric; like in the land of Oz, 'don't mind the little man behind the curtain, just look over here at the giant facade'.

If it were everywhere, available to all... If it were in you, your own natural gift - a birthright, free for the taking... Then who could profit from it?

Hmmmm....

Well!?

Why not the true source of it? Your own wonderful SELF!

While I have nothing against religion, in fact my favorite religion is kindness, please do not get confused by assigning something outside of you as the cause.

Your work is to recognize that YOU are the creator of your life. Get in harmony with that knowing.

You get to adjust your levels, nothing is set.

Rewrite your own script, act it out on the world's stage. Use your own wonderful imagination to create and re-create, as you desire. Why not be your own masterpiece?

CELEBRITY TEACHING POINTS

While I haven't won an Oscar or appeared on the cover of Vogue, I have had my own level of success. Early on, I had identified success with a fixed idea that was ultimately meaningless, instead of celebrating and recognizing the wins I was having in that moment.

When we measure ourselves against an arbitrary marker, often set up long before having any real understanding of what is deeply important, we overlook so much of what the 4th C is about. The good news, **we can celebrate retroactively.**

Don't overlook the little successes, they may not always show up the way you think.

Some of our most valuable recognitions can come from what would be mistaken as a failure.

Learn to recognize the value and re-frame what it means in terms of competition versus creation.

Don't judge something as black or white, right or wrong, win or lose, failure or success. Recognize instead, there is more room to "color outside the lines" in order to create your masterpiece.

CELEBRITY QUESTS

1. Evaluate and get crystal clear on what you want to be known for.

2. Define clearly for yourself, what it means for you to be recognized, valued, honored, and celebrated.

Give yourself a tangible benchmark, otherwise, how will you know when you've attained it?

--BONUS--

If you haven't had the chance to download the supplemental workbook at www. model4business. com/ workbook, I'll give you one more reminder. I've got a few other bonuses for you there as well!

CELEBRITY AFFIRM ACTIONS

1. Build into your daily practice: celebrating, recognizing and acknowledging the right actions along the process.

Feel appreciation for being honored for your unique gifts. Be willing and open to being seen, heard and honored, for your unique gifts, in life and business.

Avoid at all costs, seeking approval or recognition from 'likes' and the fakers, who are not in the arena doing the work.

2. Celebrate the small wins, yours as well as others.

Do the celebrating mindfully, in a way that nourishes you and your expansion. Avoid becoming narcissistic, as that is futile to C4.

Being able to recognize what you need to change or improve in your life and business along the way, and doing it, that is also worth celebrating!

3. Ask for clear feedback where it's not in alignment with your caliber of outcome, correct this, make it right then celebrate.

Through written or spoken or video communication get reviews, case studies, testimonials, and success stories and share them broadly with the public.

The Practice

FROM STUDENT TO C4 MASTERY

C4 Mastery is not a destination, it is a practice. Remember that story of the music producer who made my cat scratch voice sound rather melodious, using the levels on the mixing board?

Well, you're going to be shifting the levels on your life and business, adjusting them so they resonate harmoniously, through your own C4 Mastery!

Some people learn by seeing the whole, while others need to see each step laid out, and others like to see it all in action through examples.

I'll do my best to share with you in several ways: through practical action steps, more stories, a couple of case studies and coaching points.

It's best if you look at this as a singular methodology. Avoid trying to fit it into something else you are already doing. While there are certainly many methods you can bring in, for now, just do the steps as I've outlined. Get proficient at the C4 process and then start making it your own. By all means throw out what doesn't work for you, keep what does.

CLARITY PRACTICE ACTIONS

Identify clearly your goals for your business and your life.

Start with the big picture view. You are marking the X on your map so that you have a known destination, clearly defined with an understanding of the obstacles, potential challenges on the way, as well as clarity of purpose on why **this** destination. Then we can start working backwards to see how the process might unfold and create a strategic plan of action toward that singular point of focus with the best tactics to navigate the way.

Next, you must get clear on your framework as it relates to your goal. Think of this as getting your provisions in place, preparations for your journey, including evaluating for assets, strengths and weakness.

What does your optimal state of Energy, Work, Love and Wisdom need to be in order to achieve your current, specific goal?

Questions you want answered:

ENERGY:

Get super clear on your basics.

What time do you need to shut down the digital devices, so you can get in bed at a decent hour, so that you

get the sleep you need to get up on time?
Do you need to make changes to your diet or add in an exercise routine?
Read and research any billionaire entrepreneur and they all state these are key factors in their success.

What are the clear, simple actions you need to take daily, to ensure your energy is optimal?

Consider water, nutrition, movement, breathing, sleeping, time in nature, silent and/or meditation time, thoughts and emotions.

Get clarity on what must get done and what you will not tolerate.

Don't skip this piece as it is often the key to your success. This is also a great way to establish some healthy boundaries for the long haul, as you are faced with distractions and hurdles that come up along the route to your goal.

If you get this right, you will have a built in clarity and calm confidence to easily reinforce what works and ignore or eliminate what doesn't support you.

WORK:

When is your optimal time to do the deep work for your business?

Map out your daily time blocks based on your optimal energy outputs: organizing, handling communications, marketing, sales, finances, delivery, improving delivery methods, publicity, leading your business with strategic planning, etc.

Are you more focused in the morning?

Are you more productive later in the day?

Time block your day based on that clarity.

Remember you became an entrepreneur because YOU wanted to call the shots and work on your time.

Your schedule may not look like the typical 9-5 and that's a good thing.

LOVE:

This may seem touchy feely but I won't skimp here either. Some of my best client successes broke through major barriers after getting this one leg of the framework sorted out. This piece includes self love, as well as your family and personal relationships.

What does that look like in its optimal state?

This could look like getting a monthly or weekly massage. Taking a walk first thing in the morning or last thing at night to clear your head and reconnect to your goal. Whatever works for you, get clarity on it and put it in writing. Making the time for deep connection with your loved ones is essential. I can't tell you how many clients have tripped themselves up because they compromised in this area.

WISDOM:

Knowledge is wonderful but if you don't have understanding, it's really useless. Understanding comes from thoughtful reflection and expanding the gap of stimulus to response.

No longer will you live a life or make a business that is reactive. Level up here and your rewards are far greater and far more lasting.

At the end of each day, I suggest you look in the mirror and ask yourself what you have learned and what you still have to learn.

This simple act can provide significant clarity. Do not do this from a place of judgment, rather from a place of compassion. Connect with your higher self as you seek mastery of your highest good and best outcome for your life and business.

Of course confidence is naturally going to increase as you level up this way. And as you start living your life in this congruent, harmonious way, it will be noticeable! People will want to know what you are doing differently.

That will continue to increase your innate credibility as you walk your talk.

With your celebration of that, it will increase.

When I'm coaching a client, I will continue to ask clarifying questions as needed to provide expanding perspectives and home in on their C4 Mastery.

Here are some additional questions you might ask:

Where are you now in a relationship compared to where you want to be?

Where are you now compared to where you were last year?

This gives a perspective to gauge what actions may be ineffective or areas you might want to improve upon.

Answering the above questions for yourself, do you see **where you need to take any steps right now to address immediate issues?**

Write those down.

Then take the next strategic action.

Stephana Johnson   www.model4business.com

When I was pregnant with my first son, I was crystal clear I'd need to make significant changes to my work levels as my priority was to grow my healthy baby.

My clarity around what I needed to do for my Energy and Love in my framework leveled up and I confidently shifted my work from being on movie sets for long hours, to a dormant stage, intentionally (no guilt, no regret).

I was clear on my numbers, so shifting my focus in Work, I knew my financial bottom line and how I could bring in more revenue without compromising my overall goal.

I researched and promoted myself for maternity modeling. As my belly grew and I grew more confident in my new role, I knew I could handle more. My niche was so clear I didn't have to sell anything, instead I located the clients who needed a maternity model or actress and let them know I was available.

I signed with a specialty agency, built credibility and worked the amount I wanted, all based on my personal framework.

I was charging my day rate with no push back. In a four and half month period, I developed a level of celebrity I was comfortable with, getting referred and recognized.

I also experienced an expansion in my Wisdom as I

studied natural health as well as being fully present and in intentional through my whole pregnancy and motherhood realm.

This is an example of C4 Mastery in Practice and how you can lead a business AND life that you truly love!

FINANCIAL CLARITY QUESTIONS:

Money and finances seem to be an area that trips so many people up. I'm speaking from first hand personal experience, so let me know share some insight.

Keep in mind, I am not giving legal or accounting advice. These are just a few of the simple, intelligent questions you want to answer for yourself.

What is your bottom line number that you need to earn?

What is the cost of your doing business?

Break this down by product or service.

Knowing these numbers will also help you see at a glance what is a **viable activit**y and what needs to be jettisoned.

Factor in the cost of paying yourself, please don't forget this step!

How much money do you need to earn personally?

This is super important. You and your business finances must be separate. Trust me on this, if you don't, you will never expand in a viable way as a business and you will only resent the business sooner or later.

Pay yourself. Some say FIRST. But frankly, it took me

enjoying beans and rice for a bit while I paid for a coach to help me know what I didn't know.

Factor in costs of staff, office expenses, administrative time, legal, accounting, marketing, advertising, delivery, etc.

For every client hour I deliver, I factor in 2 hours of admin. This includes ALL admin and training.

That's something you want to know.

One can't do 40 hours of client delivery because that's actually going to amount to 120 hours of work as you factor in executive planning, sales and marketing, communications, treasury, taxes, filing, legal, quality control, learning, staying abreast of current skills, social media and public relations, etc. If you are a solo entrepreneur starting out, it might just be planning, sales, marketing, delivery but it still needs to get done.

You need and want to know this so when you scale you are clear about the actions it takes to actually deliver and run your business.

Then you'll start seeing how you can and should scale, as you start thinking in these terms from the beginning.

This isn't meant to complicate things. Believe me, as a creative, I just wanted to get in and get delivering, but as an entrepreneur, you need to understand all of these components. Even if you plan to hire most of it out.

Create a simple spreadsheet (or make it elaborate, if that's your thing) and set up a 12 month forecast of income projections and expenses.

Always look at that bottom line number - income minus outgo plus money to reserves. This will give you the data to see realistically the estimation of time and effort to be a viable, fulfilling business.

Financial clarity is of the utmost importance, and having missed this step caused the complete collapse of one of my businesses. This is a key metric and not to be skipped. I had compromised on it myself, because I was confused and didn't want to confront the numbers - to great peril. Please make sure you get and keep in your financial clarity.

I promise you, the time you take to get clarity on your numbers will pay you in dividends. Chaos of finances will have significant diminishing returns and cripple not only your business but your life.

If you are anything like me around numbers (I use to avoid the whole area), when you get clarity on your numbers, it contributes to expansion of your confidence like nothing else will. It will also simplify all your choices and remove much unnecessary stress and unwise purchases.

A few more tips before we leave this:

Always check receipts for accuracy.

Always check your credit card statements for accuracy.

Always check your P & L for accuracy.

At least once a week.

ALWAYS!

Each morning I start my day with a clarity check on where I want to go with my finances. I factor in my framework to ensure I'm optimizing each for the best results. Believe me it's not that complicated and takes moments. Because I learned the hard way, taking those couple of minutes a day and a bit longer 10-20 a week to really know your numbers, will save you weeks if not years of misery and regret.

During my pregnancies, I knew I needed to emphasize Energy; sleep and hydration were the biggest.

I went from needing 7 hours to needing 10+ a night and a nap during the day. Understanding this, I could keep things in harmony and created a truly blissful pregnancy and childbirth without extra stress.

I approached my whole business from a new point of clarity as I became a mom.

Take a few moments each day to set your clarity for the day and align your actions. This daily re-alignment is leverage for your success and to keep you from burning out.

There will be different phases in your life, where there will be significant spikes in one area or the other.

Life happens - that's a good thing.

The most important thing to understand is that you want to address your current situational framework from this place of awareness as you practice C4 Mastery.

Stephana Johnson   www.model4business.com

CASE STUDY ANALYSIS

This is an actual example of C4 Mastery action steps I personally made to go from a 0 to 6 figure revenue for a brick and mortar service based business over an 8 month period of time.

GOAL: Our goal is to educate the public on optimal movement, mindset and nutrition as it effects overall quality of life.

We accomplish this by promoting and selling programs and services which help our clients eliminate pain without pills and surgery and improve our clients lives while building a viable expanding global organization.

PURPOSES: To make a positive difference in the lives of our clients and their families by promoting and selling optimal movement, mindset and nutrition programs

To develop and broadly market products which help our clients understand and choose optimal movement, mindset and nutrition as a solution to pain and ultimately a lifestyle choice To develop and broadly market the programs as a resource for positive change within our community and expanding to planet wide.

POLICY: Maintain consistent congruent branding in all of our communication.

Send out a weekly newsletter communication to every person in our database.

Hire team members who are genuinely interested in the mission and purpose

STRATEGIC PURPOSEFUL PLANNING:

Big Dream:

1000 Studios globally with 100+ VIP members in each studio

11,000+ members learning and practicing optimal movement, mindset and nutrition daily.

1000 master trainers certified and well paid running successful studios in their community

TARGET MARKET:

Busy professionals 35 and over in a 6-10 mile radius of each studio. They are repulsed by box gyms and cookie cutter approaches, have the desire and ability to invest in private training and personal expert holistic guidance toward optimal well being.

Milestone 1: Open first studio!

PROGRAMS: (each step was then broken down in to programs and mini projects, some of which were delegated)

Design and Build website and marketing collateral.

Secure studio space.

Secure licenses and all logistical documentation.

Handle any legal basics, trademarks, taxes, contracts, client documentation, insurance, etc.

Establish accounts - general, saving, tax, payroll.

STRATEGIC PLAN PHASE 1

One month prior to grand opening, run beta testing classes and streamline systems from each touch point to final product delivered, success story collected and corrected as needed*

IDEAL VISION:

A thriving community of coaches and members in a viable, expanding organization with well paid staff and reserves to open multiple studios each year. Making a positive impact on the lives of 10,000+ members each day.

KEY METRICS:

Number of Active VIP Members

Number of New Members

Gross Revenue from Memberships, Services, Programs and Products.

Tracked separately as well.

Corrected Gross Revenue (Gross Income - Bills + Reserves)

Well trained Staff Members

New Names Added to Database

Based on initial studio opening, document process and what needs to be done in order to coordinate and keep the business producing, viable and expanding

***Beta testing** is an excellent way to introduce your services to the community while also going through your processes to streamline for efficacy. I highly recommend doing beta testing with all of your products and services. It can provide so much data for improvement and it takes the pressure off if you have to pivot or scrap some part of your methodology or systems.

Once you work out any bugs and are ready to launch,

you can do so with much higher confidence. Your credibility will already be increasing as a bonus!

Follow some of the publicity action steps I share later, and you will increase your credibility and celebrity right along with your confidence and clarity during your beta tests.

Getting excited?

Now it's your turn!

Get your notebook out and work on your own strategic planning.

CONFIDENCE PRACTICE ACTIONS

The way to get confidence is to ensure you have clear plans for your business before you do anything that requires long-term commitments. Like signing a 5 or 10 year lease.

This may seem redundant, but it's key to your confidence.

Now that you've written down your plans, let's review them. Do these plans align with your life purpose and current levels of framework?

What does the delivery plan for your business look like? Are you going to deliver or outsource? Will it be in person or on line? Do you need training or to improve the delivery of your product or service?

Begin executing your strategic plans. I mentioned the beta testing above. I love this as a tactic for building confidence. My clients and I have saved countless months of time and headache by testing something before putting everything "in stone".

Gain confidence by working through and working out the bugs before "going live". Every time I have clients use this strategy and they invite their list to a beta test, they inevitably increase their bottom line, gain confidence and clarity and get even more credibility. Clients love when a business takes the time to test and evaluate. Showing you are interested in their honest feedback and improving outcomes, boosts **their** confidence!

Above all, ensure delivery of your products and services get completed. If you promise to deliver something, make it happen.

Failing this is the fastest way to lose credibility. It's also a poor show of confidence. I do not agree with the concept widely promoted by many coaches to "sell it before you even know what you are going to deliver". That's for people who really don't know what they are doing. By all means, do the beta test, but don't BS your way through business.

Once you have your plan, stay with it long enough to get results, one way or the other. A ninety day plan is short, but will give you metrics. With the numbers, you can confidently predict what's working and what need to be changed.

This is another big pitfall I see with clients - they go rogue and lose sight of their ultimate plan, adding a lot of extra frustration to their path by getting distracted with all the other pretty courses out there.

If you want the compound effect of C4, building some explosive momentum, stay the course.

As you increase your confidence, both internally and externally, set up plans for expansion. Make time for evaluating your overall plans, ensuring clear doable steps, even if it means you need to level way up in the Wisdom department by apprenticing with an expert.

When you start looking at things from this viewpoint, building a successful business and life, it is enjoyable, fulfilling and profitable!

Through the clarity steps you now have a clearly defined business, making it easier for you to get found, hired, referred and celebrated.

Doesn't that make you feel more confident?

FINE TUNING

At this point you should have written down what you do, in terms of what solution, transformation, result or outcome you provide. Now, who do you provide that for? Let's get this fine tuned.

Who do you really love providing that for?
Describe them in detail: do they pay on time?
How old or young?
Where do they live, shop, eat, get their hair and nails done?
Do they have kids, pets?
What charities do they support?

All of this is intelligence gathering and fosters increased clarity and confidence.

What does your ideal client suffer most from, in their words?

What sound bites or images do they use and respond to, that YOU are the expert solution to?

You will be positioning your business in the eyes of your ideal market from a place of confident and congruent messaging, penetrating the masses and differentiating yourself as the absolute best choice!

And with that kind of confidence, it makes the selling piece a whole lot different.

Let's raise your confidence level even more.

Here's an overall framework your business needs to be doing to function at all:

ATTRACTING CLIENTS: What forms of communication will you use?

Visual, written or video (newsletter, articles, website, blog, signage, photos, graphics, images, video)
Verbal (speaking, podcasts, webinar, colleges, trade school, conventions, association meetings)

What is most aligned with your brand and stays congruent?

CAPTURE CONTACTS: Collecting contact information so you can develop the relationship.

Most information today is email and name, but I like to mail a hard copy newsletter and I will also mail birthday cards.

Capture their information both in person, if you have a brick and mortar or on line. Here are some effective ways to capture: through a newsletter subscription, consult request form, contest entry (naming contest, best photo, etc), free class, free offer, low barrier offer, application (employment, consulting, speaking request, etc.)

NURTURE: Through high quality, brand congruent points of contact with your clients and target market, you will build confidence in you/ your business at every touch point.

Examples are: email a regular newsletter, direct mail newsletter/magazine, an open house, monthly or quarterly subscriber/client appreciation, video of the week, tip of the week, etc.

FINANCES: Accounting and finances are not the same thing. You will want to consult a professional in handling your accounting and books. But finances, this is different than accounting. This is how you are going to collect payments, credit card processing, bill paying, banking, allocations, book keeping, taxes and legal agreements, etc.

All part of your business. You'll need to get clarity on this area, it's often the weak link that eats away confidence for entrepreneurs.

I also suggest a weekly financial planning session to ensure your business is viable. This is where you sit down and get clear on your numbers. Keep this as a regular action as you expand with staff, because as the business owner, you must always maintain a pulse on your numbers.

CONVERT/HIRE: Always have a CTA or call to action. Either be making proposals or offers or directing your audience to a clear next step action.

As you expand you will need to set up systems for your team building, educating/training process, interview process, sales process.

ON BOARDING: Growing and developing your team and leaders is crucial bu. I find clients do better with an on boarding process as well.

Welcome them with written, verbal, on brand contact. Stream line this as a key piece to foster confidence and build credibility with your clients (as well as your team!) When this gets sloppy it shows up as a source of a lot of other issues. It's one area, that if you invest in wisely, cuts out a lot of issues down the line.

DELIVERY: Rock star delivery to your clients, and exceptional delivery within your organization from team members to you and vise versa.

All around rock star delivery makes for awesome production and a much easier expansion. First policy should always be to deliver what you promise. Ensure product downloads, quality editing, quality design, etc.

There will always be iterations. Be sure to have a system that works for you to identify the latest iterations so you are not doubling your work load.

ONGOING TRAINING & DEVELOPMENT:

Always be improving.

I spend 1-2 hours of personal development and relevant training per week but when I am learning a new platform more is needed. Find out what is ideal for you to always be improving.

Each team member needs to know the current big focus and be self reliant in improving their own skills toward it's attainment. Confidence within the team increases client confidence. Have on going, scheduled and dedicated training time.

Some of the areas I've had to add in when I was hiring interns, included eye contact, listening and basic people skills, never assume someone knows the fundamentals of common courtesy.

We live in a different age with texting and distraction overload. This will literally kill a business if someone is on your "front lines" and doesn't have the basic skills to communicate. Never put someone on your first point of contact that hasn't been trained well and qualified by YOUR clear standards.

Time must be blocked out on the calendar and adhered to so that you are always improving. If you aren't, believe me, you will become irrelevant and your income will diminish.

QUALITY CONTROL AND CORRECTION:

One thing I see missing in a lot of businesses, is a checks and balances for quality control. It may come from the fast pace, churn and burn, mass 'quantity over quality' mentality. Use the "debrief" as a skill for yourself and your team to always be leveling up.

While I wouldn't focus on the negative comments, do take the time to find out when there is a situation and get it corrected. Whatever that means for your business. While you don't need to offer refunds, I do suggest you make good on what you promise. You'll want to address this at the level of your business, internally as well as externally.

PUBLICITY & PUBLIC RELATIONS

We'll go deeper into this soon, but know that it's a part of your overall organizational structure. I enjoy hosting parties for my clients and celebrating them, whether on their birthdays or for milestones in life or business. These are "publicity" opportunities.

Build in a system for referrals so your clients know that you appreciate their feedback and their referrals. It doesn't have to be monetary, although it can be.

Whatever you decide, make it part of your business operations.

QUICK CONFIDENCE BOOSTERS

At least once a week clean off your desk, clean up your office, clean out your purse. Make it an official confidence boosting and 'releasing' ritual.

When you get to your office (even if it's a desk in your bedroom) pull out your plan. I use a 3 ring binder with everything in one place, it's my "CAPCOM" or Control Center. Review it, update it, follow it. Keep all of your above protocols and policy in this binder. It will help start and end your day with intentional clarity and confidence.

Sometimes you need to create quick action steps to get small (and sometimes massive) wins. Create a go to list of items or actions you can take that require little time and effort but get quick wins.

What are some things you can do that are efficient and get you one step closer to where you want to be? At the top of my list is a personal phone call to past and current clients, or top affiliates. This often leads to a new client, a referral and increase in revenue, as it puts you and your business 'top of mind'.

Be realistic in your expectations of yourself and others.

Practice patience and be your own best friend. Do the right things at the right time and you will get the results.

Let's face it, we can get knocked off our game. Here are some additional DIY tools I share with my clients and apply myself:

When feeling bad, for whatever reason, do NOT go on social media. Step away from the computer/ detach from your phone. Take a breath and relax your shoulders. Get a drink water. Step away from the task and take a short walk.

If you've done the above and are still feeling bad, take one drawer, or your purse, or a shelf and clean it out.

If still feeling bad, wash the dishes with warm soapy water, rinse, dry and put them away.

Still? Sweep the front walk way and wash the front door - both home and if you have a brick and mortar.

Still? Wash the windows, scrub the bath tub, the toilet, then fold and put away laundry. This tip was from an academy award winning actress who said it's her way of getting things back in perspective. I loved it when I learned it from her 20 years ago, and love it still!

Is it a distraction? Some think it is, but it's far better than social media or other nefarious kryptonite to your C4 Mastery. At least putting your house in order is helping! When you do this, your energy, confidence and vitality should return and you can get back at it, in tact.

(One side note on "feeling bad" - as a trained cognitive therapist, I am not saying to ignore the pain or feeling, in fact, it is information and in the right time and place, should get addressed. Stay alert and be willing to experience the pain or sensation fully, so you can learn where it's actually coming from. But don't identify yourself as "it". Ideally you want to get to the source of the discomfort and eliminate it at the roots, getting the valuable message in the process.)

This has never failed to get me back in action and my clients rave about my simple house keeping rules to restore confidence. The clean environment is a nice side effect.

Ultimately, what we want, is to shorten that time spent in self doubt, chaos or confusion, and bridge that gap to being whole, present, in harmony and back to clarity and confidence as quickly as possible. Then you can do the next best and right thing.

BOUNDARIES

A key point for home offices, but absolutely applies to workplace offices, you must set strict boundaries for your energy and deep work time. Do not allow yourself to be distracted constantly, whether by family interruptions or on-line interruptions.

This may seem innocuous, but it etches away at our focus and creates diminishing returns. For your deep work time, put the phone on do not disturb mode and don't have it near you. Close your email. Close all windows and tabs but the one/s you are using, specifically.

Communicate in advance with family members or co-workers that you are in your "FOCUS" time. You can create a sign and inform people in your environment that when it is set to "ON AIR" (in session, etc. as you prefer), that they are not to interrupt for ANY reason - well OK, if the place is on fire. But otherwise, deep Work time is sacred.

DECIDE TO BE CONFIDENT

Decide to be successful.
Decide to be happy.
Decide to be beautiful.
Decide to be healthy.
Decide to be in love - with yourself, with life, with your children, with your lover, with your business!
Decide to be rich and wealthy and abundant.

If you aren't making decisions, you are making excuses.

Decide to be Confident.

TAKE PERSONAL RESPONSIBILITY

Take personal responsibility... for your money, for your time, for your thoughts, for your actions, for your emotions, for your habits, for your past, for your present for your future.

Take personal responsibility for your health, your wealth, your success, your power, your energy, your outcomes.

And never ever relegate it to someone or something else again. Ever.

FIND YOUR FINANCIAL FREEDOM NUMBER

Carefully consider every expenditure.

Ask yourself serious questions about everything:

Is this expenditure really necessary? Or is it possible to get the same personal effect without using money? Or using less of it?

Is this expenditure contributing to my wealth? Will this expenditure bring me profit? I'm not talking just monetary profit - but profit in your energy, love and wisdom too.

Is this an impulse purchase or a planned purchase?

Am I being pressured to make an expenditure I'm not certain about? Do I feel I have to justify this expenditure?

All of these can give you more confidence in making decisions, when you ask and answer from a healthy place.

Freedom and power are far better than momentary pleasure. And far too many people spend money they haven't earned, to buy things they don't really need or even want, to impress people that really mean nothing to their well being. I know this has been said many different ways, whatever way it's stated, it has truth.

Do not ever equate spending money with your happiness. As a parent, avoid at all costs, wrapping spending money into happiness for your children.

Foster gratitude and appreciation as a key confidence strategy to buying things you don't need.

Evaluate whether the person you trust to do your books or handle your investments is sufficiently skilled to handle your money. Then always know your own numbers and what they mean.

Make sure you have the proper legal structures in place early on. Insurance. Agreements. Contracts. Insurance. Do you want to put your assets in Trusts? LLC? Corporate documents? Keep your documents current and simple. If you don't understand something, ask a trustworthy source or learn about it. Don't leave this area unhandled, as the longer you go, the unknown and fear will hold you back from sustainable success.

Know your financial freedom number. Financial freedom means all of your expenses are covered by passive income. Knowing this number, and not having some arbitrary "to be a millionaire" number is key to confidence, especially when you realize you are a lot closer than you think!

Did you know that if you saved just $100 a month in the S&P 500 (10%) within forty years it could be worth 700K?

PUTTING A PRICE ON WORTHINESS

When I started out in coaching, I had done a lot for free. That's a tell tale sign of an amateur, no doubt. But I had been taught to give free discovery sessions and already had a giving mentality. So it backfired as I gave more and more away for free and cut my prices when someone couldn't afford my services.

Ideally, you now have the clarity and confidence as an expert and know exactly what your prices need to be. There should be no reason to discount. EVER.

Give bonuses by all means, but do NOT discount. This immediately diminishes your C4.

If you wish to give something for free or choose to do a certain amount of pro bono work, do so from a place of integrity with yourself. Be clear that it is Bono as a PRO, and document it.

Remember, keep giving it away, and nobody is going to benefit.

On the other hand, don't do the ridiculous and put out made up, inflated prices, especially on your freebies. We've all seen the gimmick, 'get $50,000 worth...when you...' That lacks integrity and is the marketing manipulation game that wreaks of slimy tactics.

That's instant diminished credibility in my book.

Here's a few other ideas on pricing your goods and services:

If your pricing is such that you resent the work, it's too low.

If it's priced that people are on a wait list, it's too low.

If it's priced and folks are not buying because it's beneath them and seems too cheap, it's too low.

Here's what I've learned, from major billion dollar corporations to Beverly Hills designers to a yoga class - pricing is relative and it's all subjective.

You have to know 2 key numbers - cost of doing business and client acquisition. Then figure out your margin. More on this later.

When I first heard about my coach paying her coach $100K, yes, that's one hundred thousand dollars, for a year long group coaching program, with a 30 minute monthly session with the coach, I just honestly thought, that chick is stupid.

But you know what, she made her first million the next year. She said it forced her necessity level to come up. She'd "either have to make the money or die". Her words. That idea just doesn't work for me and it may not be your thing either. But here's what I do know from investing in my own coaches and mentors in every area I've wanted to level up in and master - you have to know what the ROI (return on investment) ultimately can be. However, if I can't see where it will bring me real profit back (remember profit can be fulfillment, better energy, love, work, wisdom) it's a simple equation.

I've had a salesperson ask me "what would you do if kidnappers had your child? You'd find the money right?" She was a dog with a bone salesperson and I gave her far more credibility than she came by honestly. I despise this type of "sales" and it's not good for anyone.

I don't like that game and I wish for us all to be confident enough to call people out on it. I don't need to pay someone $100K to make me work under pressure. At the same time, I'd happily pay a consultant $25K to provide me a 20+% ROI on my investment.

The numbers can often be arbitrary these days. But the bottom line, is still the number you want. If you can't see a direct correlation in your investment, whether of time, money, attention, energy or action, remove it.

If spending your time posting on social media gets you clients, awesome, by all means get on that. But always look at the numbers.

The two key metrics to track:

What is the cost of each client acquisition?

What is the lifetime value of each client?

Know this and you can clearly design viable marketing, advertising, publicity and PR campaigns.

Don't look at what the market will bear, look at your margins. Yes, there are some "standards", especially for brick and mortar businesses, because there is a much bigger overhead here.

Rule of thumb, your rent should be no more than 10% of your revenue. Payroll is usually 30-35% and 40-45% to marketing and operations. That leaves 10-20% for reserves and an emergency fund.

The process of raising your clarity comes from knowing your numbers, not guessing or assuming.

For solo entrepreneurs who work from home, often you have financial freedom at a much lower level. Depending on what you value in terms of lifestyle and expenses, you'll factor that in for yourself.

I'm all for luxury and niceties but I am an environmentalist at heart. I think there is a tremendous amount of waste and greed that is not sustainable. Without getting on a soap box, I'll say this, know what your bottom line number is, every day.

Know your financial baseline: total income minus total outgo and the spread between the two. These numbers should not cross. If they do, you are insolvent.

When you can see this at a glance and you have your previous steps in place, you can very quickly turn things around.

You are in business to make a profit (among other things of course) and have a viable, expanding organization.

Get expert at the numbers.

Everyone needs to learn to basic money math money, income and expenditures, ideally at an early age.

Do an audit on your books, or have someone do them with you until you can understand the importance for yourself. Understanding your numbers is the key to bringing simplicity to finances.

Set yourself up for the real reason most of us go into business for ourselves - freedom, that means financially, as well as time!

I'm a stickler now for tracking results. Even in coaching, whether I am giving or receiving. I want results and an ROI for myself and my business. And I want to make sure my clients get an ROI. So far my baseline has been a 30% ROI for my clients in my 90 day programs and it usually happens by week 6.

Now why would I track that? You guessed it. It builds not only clarity of "am I doing the right things at the right time with my clients", but confidence, for myself as an effective expert, as well as for my clients and potential clients increased confidence!

This then leads to that credibility piece. Clients can see in black and white the results. They trust the process. They trust the results and they become your best referral source. Sharing you, sharing your business.

Getting celebrated and invited to speak to your ideal audience or interviewed as the expert in your field is a natural part of that process.

Are you starting to see how C4 is weaving through everything?

NOTHING IS SET IN STONE

Circumstances, situations and "states" are not fixed. They can be used as a gauge and adjusted as needed. Now that you understand how to start aligning within your framework, you can create more harmonic levels, just like what that producer using the mixing board, did for my voice!

Does knowing some of this take some of the guess work out of where you have been spending your time, money, and attention? Does it give you a clue as to what you need to eliminate and what you need to focus more on?

I want to say one more thing on the topic of "charging what you are worth" . There are a lot of coaches who go after this with a vengeance. I don't believe "charging what you're worth" is at the root cause of a business challenge.

Let's just shine some light on the lies on money and worthiness right now. In many coaching and speaking business models, selling from the stage with radical scarcity and competition is a key tactic; hijacking your attention with confiscatory pricing.

It is not new, it's been around for centuries. I don't play that way and it's not in harmony with C4 Mastery.

In all of my time, with all of the clients I've worked with, there is never a cookie cutter solution or strategy. The C4 work can't be skimped on by the individuals themselves. That's what I've been trying to share with you throughout this book.

No matter where you are right now, I believe it's exactly where you need to be. When it comes to up leveling your clarity and confidence to find your C4 Mastery, all of your experiences are potential information.

Whatever is happening right now; whether you are bankrupt or trying to break your first million, there is a unique tuning that matches up with you, and you have to do the work to find it.

For certain, I can help facilitate along the way, but I'm not going to do the work for you. You have to show up, face what there is to face. Of course, that's not the only step, but it's the first and often the most difficult.

The clients you are here to serve will value your services and products. Willingly paying your prices, because through your C4 Mastery practice, you will have made yourself and your business invaluable as the clear expert with an irresistible offer that solves your markets problem.

There will always be someone who devalues your products, service and time. Remember the story of the entourage and fakers? There will always be those who will tear others down, thinking in doing so, it makes them mightier.

Ultimately however, we are all in this together and we all only get out together.

Bottom line, who is looking back at you at night when you stand in front of the mirror to brush your teeth?

If you can't look straight in your eyes and say, "I love you and everything you stand for", you've got bigger issues than charging what you are worth. Get after that one in a big way, it's a major stumbling block.

Again, you've got to know your numbers. **ALWAYS.**

I have a daily monitoring system that is a simple piece of paper with "Income in the door" across the top. It's become my target to write a dollar amount, down to the penny, daily. Every single day. This one simple action boosted my confidence around my own value and shifted my mindset taking scarcity off of the numbers. These checks and balances, done regularly, keep you on target to your goal. I'm an ultra minimalist, so I do things pretty simply and my financial planning documents amount to columns on one spreadsheet.

Whatever way you decide to do this, get it done and be precise. Be like the scientist, or an unattached observer looking at the numbers. They tell you something. Don't get caught up in the emotions that confuse your money energy. This is a piece I go deeper on with my clients, but it's not the scope of this book. If you need more help on the energy and emotion around money, visit www.stephanajohnson.com for a course that addresses this at its roots.

PRETTY LITTLE PACKAGES

One of my first coaches taught about creating your 'signature system'. This is still workable and I'm going to expand on it with you here. But I want you to understand that this is not a complicated step when you have been practicing C4 Mastery.

Like a low end restaurant with a large unfocused menu, having a list of services you can do is not the way to separate yourself out from your competition.

A past client who had an arms length list of services he could deliver came to me for private coaching. On the surface he looked like everything was peachy. But after we looked under the hood, what was found was an unfocused, chaotic business model with big revenue goals but daily self doubt and self sabotage that showed up as significant distractions and excuses.

He was overworked, underpaid. His physical health was a disaster and his personal life was in turmoil. He was doing countless, random, foolish actions and was out of integrity with himself and his staff.

He let his clients run the show, even though they didn't

pay on time. On top of it all, he was part of several high end mastermind coaching programs, even being a featured coach in that group, while he was a hot mess.

Sadly, this is a whole lot more common than not. And I want you to get how serious this is. Please, **do not** ever again compare your back room to someone's front yard.

What people put out on social media or what you see in their "front yards", is rarely what's really going on inside.

It's my mission in life to transform this, so we are whole, from the inside out.

So back to my client. For years, he had been operating as a victim from false wisdom and confusion. This too, is not uncommon, and without getting into personal details, his framework was completely broken. By sorting it at the foundation, cleaning up his Energy, Work, Love and Wisdom, he nearly instantly had new found clarity and confidence. Before the week was out, he literally looked like a different person. In under ten days, he had collected over $15K in past fees due and brought in an additional $30K in new revenue. Our next session, we looked at what he actually did for his clients. He was able to see exactly where his expertise was and to stop giving away his time because he felt guilty. We cleared that and he was able to articulate in one sentence exactly how he changed his clients lives. He was so clear that he could easily identify exactly who needed and wanted it and would pay gladly. That became his core offering. He figured out how many he needed to sell to be viable and how it would be delivered with his teams which made it something he could scale. He had an exact road map to his multi-million dollar revenue goal, with the clarity and confidence to achieve it and is now on his way for real. With a fabulous, happy relationship and a healthier body as an aligned "bonus"!

Your expertise, compiled into the result you get, for your ideal client, is your attention grabbing, signature system, bullseye product.

You do NOT need a multi page menu of services. That just sets you up to be a 'jack of all' general service provider.

From there, you can make a small and a medium size package that aligns with your business and supports your clients steps to success.

Do you remember those "free discovery sessions" ? That's my small offer and what I suggest you use as your low barrier offer.

Once you have C4 Mastery, your time is NOT free.

So let's say you've got a potential client or a new person who has walked in. They are looking around your "store" and see that you have a widget for sale. But it's a little too small for their needs, so they'll look at the large, but that's a little much. Ah, but the medium is just right. This can also be said but having an up-sell or a down-sell for clients, but no more 10 page menu of a la carte services.

Really, it's not too much more complicated than that and it shouldn't be made ANY more complicated. Do not have a menu of things to fit everybody's potential problems. Be the expert with your main product offering and a small and medium version.

The only people that want a menu of offerings are the people that are usually looking for the cheapest item on the menu, not getting their problem solved.

If you want to eliminate a huge headache of sales, then get this step done right.

OK, one more time in a paragraph:

What does your main product solve?

That's your OFFER.

Who does it solve it for?

That's your MARKET

Now, start having conversations with the people who need and want that SOLUTION or the companies that have the problem that you Solve. Package a small, medium and large, sometimes XL.

Go to it!

GETTING SUPPORT

There are times when one has a problem but doesn't know what it is - could be health, personal, professional or other facets of life. Perhaps you just don't know how to find it, nor fix it. Recognizing when you are off, in either personal or professional life, is a credibility point for all of us, because you need to be able to depend on yourself to show up fully and lead the life you are here to lead. Indeed, we all need support. But the right support is crucial, and at the right time.

You now know to look at your overall framework, so if one area is off, it effects the whole. If you need help pinpointing what's creating the stop or slow down in your overall success, that's when you get support.

Find the expert coach or consultant. Reach out to me. This is an act of C4 Mastery. It is, in fact, one of the most credible actions you can take. I always celebrate my clients for taking that action, because it means they have outgrown their old framework. The fact that you are ready for expansion is indeed very much worth celebrating.

CELEBRITY PRACTICE ACTIONS

Let's define 'celebrity' for our purposes here. I know it can make people uncomfortable, but it's something you want to get a handle on.

Look at these concepts and notice if something comes up for you when you ask:

What if I were...

Celebrated?
Celebrating?
Well Known?
Well Thought of?
Loved?
Recognized?
Shared?
Admired?
Visible?
Valuable?
Honored?
Priceless?

And on the other spectrum-

What if I were...

Not cared about?
An outcast?

Invisible?
Not Seen?
Not Heard?
Not Understood?
Unrecognized?
Repulsive?
Hiding?
Hidden?
Embarrassed?
Discovered to be a fraud?

This "celebrity" thing can get sticky, but I hope I've given you enough insight into the reality that, it's really just a tool. How you use it is up to you.

We likely all have our own squeamish emotions that go along with the levels "From Unknown to Celebrity" .

Remember though, you are not a condition or circumstance. You now can use any condition, emotion, situation or circumstance as a way to gain clarity which in turn builds confidence, that leads to genuine credibility, and interweave the process of natural, lasting celebrity.

It's all part of the framework.

Looking at where you are on the above 'levels', from the big picture perspective, what needs work? Sometimes we need to go back to the clarity or confidence steps and tweak there. If you are ready to get more visible, the rest of this section will guide you.

PUBLIC RELATIONS

Getting publicity can increase confidence, credibility and celebrity. So let's get ready for it.

For our purposes, public relations is how you show up to the public. It's our relationship in the minds of the public. Generally, you want to be well known and well thought of in your area of expertise.

You want to be known, liked, and trusted. Sure, you want to be celebrated, recognized, shared, and honored as the respected expert in your field, by peers, as well as your ideal target market. But it's not just in the news or through media channels, although we'll get to that. It's about how well known and well thought of, you are (or your business and it's representatives are) when you show up everywhere: at your front desk, when you answer the phone, how your website and social media presence looks, etc.

You want to be consistent and congruent throughout all of your messaging and marketing, whether written, verbal, visual, etc.

Media is different than 20 years ago, and even 2 months ago. It changes with every new app. The most important thing you need to keep abreast of is who and what your target market goes to for authority.

Where do they get their news or information from?

Who do they listen to?
What are they reading?

Go on an intelligence gathering mission and find out from your top clients who they trust.

This information is gold and you want to keep it in an ongoing document with sound bites, resources and pertinent data so you can use it through your overall marketing and PR strategy.

CREATE A SIMPLE MEDIA KIT

Here is a simple structure and action steps I have my clients do to build credibility and celebrity on TV, Radio, in Print and Online.

1. Research and get in touch with (and stay in touch) your top 10 media outlets, locally and/ or regionally and tell them about you and your business:

My name is...

I am an expert in...

The relevant facts are...

I have 3 tips on A. B. C.

Contact me at ...

Reporters, like Celebrities, are people too and they want a direct and easy path to a reliable source.

Make it super easy for them. Be clear and be honest. Don't be a pest and don't ramble. Treat them with respect and kindness. With this simple strategy, you'll be amazed at the results.

Have your marketing collateral and PR materials ready to go.

This is your Media Kit: All professionally formated in your brand.

BIO (200 to 400 word bio in a word document and PDF)

Have an excellent, professional, current photo.

Or have a series of photos if you do specialty. For example, if you are a dynamic culinary expert, have an animated shot of you in your kitchen with your fabulous food. No cell phone selfies - ever. That is instant amateur hour and will take you down in credibility fast.

Sound bites (about 9 seconds of a written segment, quote or quip or a video or audio snippet) that lend credibility to you and your business.

List of your speaking topics
List of top questions an interview can ask
List of top 10 reasons to hire you
Quotes from you
Media credits
Your credentials
Experiences
Awards
Testimonials

Make a nice document and keep it current. You can even have a page on your website for potential clients or event planners or the media to download this from your site. Important if you get a lot of speaking inquiries!

THE PRESS RELEASE

I personally like sending out press releases, but it's not for everyone. It is still my first action when I have something new or big to share. With a relevant topic and an excellent hook, you can usually get 2-3 reporters calling for an interview. With your own follow up actions, it can lead to long terms relationships with news outlets and reporters that pay off in a big way. First answer these questions:

Why is your news worth celebrating?
Is it local, national?
Relevant?
Timely?

Check the calendar and look for relevancy with upcoming annual events or dates, holidays, etc. that you can position you or your business with.

Is there a HOOK?

Can you piggy back on breaking news?

Depending on what business or industry you are in, you can also actively put yourself in the spot light.

How about photo ops at local events? Premiers? Releases? Grand Openings? Screenings?

Get a press release out on you showing up with the

Stephana Johnson   www.model4business.com

mayor or with the box office star in town shooting a film?

PITCHING TO REPORTERS

Once you have your Media Kit together, start pitching. When you create a pitch letter for a reporter, do a bit of research to know how they like to be communicated with. Doing this few minutes of research on the reporters who write on your topics such as reading their articles, following up with a comment, or letting them know you liked or appreciated their article builds a connection.

You could comment and let them know you'd be happy to provide helpful insight as the leading expert on the industry or topic. Build rapport and find out what they need or want and how they prefer to be contacted.

Does your business or your expertise address a controversial subject as the solution?

Are you wanting to fuel a hot topic to position yourself as the expert?

Here are some resources for pitching:

reporterconnection.com
pitchrate.com
helpareporter.com
bloggerlinkup.com

You can even get on a podcast. That's been an easy one for me and my clients lately. There seems to be one going every minute of the day and most are wanting guests. If this is a strong venue for you, go after it with gusto. Just ensure you have clarity on how it fits into your framework and how you will be using it to level up your C4. Otherwise, honestly, it's all a waste of your time.

PITCHING TO TV

This is when you have something visual to share, like a big event or crowds happening.

I'm a global climate advocate and volunteer locally. When I led a rally of over a hundred people in Vancouver, I shared it locally to the press. Two reporters came, one with the local network affiliate with camera and crew and other for the local paper.

Our message was congruent with my own personal and business values and I shared that openly with the reporters. We made some loud, positive noise, landing on the local news that night. I had people calling me up and inquiring about my business because I was congruent about health and wellness and an advocate for a healthy environment.

This resonated with my target market and increased my C4. It wasn't my intention going in, but because I have clarity and alignment in my framework, and thus it is a natural side effect. I had people calling me to say "I saw you on channel 4 ABC news, that was amazing!" I was a celebrity in their eyes and I spread an important message.

RADIO HEAD

I like radio. It's easy and most DJs are super cool and it's fun practice public speaking without worrying about your hair. There are hundreds of stations that do interviews. You could do 10 interviews in a week and drive a lot of traffic to your site or cause, especially if you have a new launch. I was booked on over a dozen radio shows, most were 5 minute spots, and it drove my ratings out the roof for a launch of my Finding Joy Beyond Trauma book, long before the #metoo movement.

I was able to help a lot of people get useful resources on sexual trauma and abuse. Once again, it lends more credibility and celebrity itself, because it was congruent with my own framework. Starting to make sense?

PRINT/ONLINE

I also love print or online articles because you can go deeper with your message. My full length articles have been featured in startupnation.com, Huffingtonpost.com and thriveglobal.com and I suggest you submit your relevant articles to them as well. They are easy to work with. Post the article to your own blog and share all around, include link backs and calls to action that are congruent with your current strategic plans.

Use your keywords and links to your site and other articles to keep the circle. Make sure your site is current and can capture leads. You will be driving traffic organically without spending a dime.

By the way, do you know what your keywords are? They are what people are searching for to find out about your business or expertise. The more clear the better. Keep a running list of your keywords and aim for 5 in every article or blog post.

Publishing articles on line is easy and lasting. And now, it's more easy than ever to publish your own book! I have published seven books after clients asked for my notes after events and it's now very easy to do print on demand, making useful reference material for my clients and prospects.

NETWORKING EVENTS

When I was starting out, I went to a lot of networking events and joined a networking group called BNI. It was invaluable to starting my business. While it's not something I do often now, if you have decided this action is an effective tactic as part of your overall strategy, implement these key guidelines to maximize networking as a worthwhile and valuable tactic.

Always ask yourself (and as you grow make sure your

team asks this):

Why am I going this event? For what purpose?

Who will be there that I know I need and want to connect with?

What do I want to achieve? Name 1 specific outcome.

How will I measure success? Make sure this is tangible and connected to your overall goal.

Remember there is no neutral - something is either helpful or harmful - no neutrals anymore. If you could be doing something that is more effective with your time, you want that kind of clarity. Wasting a couple of hours on something that everybody else is doing because they don't have their own C4 in place, is not for you. But if you are clear that it is part of your strategy, then with the above questions answered, take the next steps.

What prep work do I need to do?

Then there are repetitive actions like:

How will I follow up? Thank you note? Call? Email?

How will I record this?

You always want to be adding to your database, but it's

quality over quantity when it comes to your contacts.

All of this takes time, so you want to be clear that it's in alignment with your overall goal and can directly contribute to your metrics. Otherwise, it's just another piece of random busy work we want to eliminate from our life.

I can't stress this enough. Please don't go to another networking event without the above done. I've had 100s of business cards from people I've met over the years, just sitting in a box after getting home from another networking event. These are distractions that could become a full time waste of your time, so get clear first. Always.

SPEAKING

Even if you don't plan to be a speaker as part of your strategy, as an expert, you will want to be quoted and be seen. Having key pieces like the basic media kit in place will increase your personal confidence when you are asked. You will also never have to race at the last minute to get something together when you start to "get found".

We already talked a bit about the Media Kit, but I'll go a little deeper on how I coach my clients to create one.

First, having high quality, excellent, professional headshots as well as 'in your element' current photos is imperative.

I like my clients to have 2-5 options for their media page and to include landscape and square, to give options. Have an option with a white background as these are often requested. Make sure you designate a high resolution photo for print media.

You will also want to have a congruent professional shot sized specially for the web for your profile and expert pages, so it doesn't get stretched or squashed when inserted in a set frame.

With your bio, don't get pedantic and tell your whole life story. Have a 200 word bio and a slightly longer bio, 400 words max. Customize your bio for introductions or for a speaking engagement specific to the audience or topic. Use and shift words as needed to connect with your audience. For example, when I am hired to speak to audiences on trauma and resiliency, I have a specific bio that connects on an emotional level with more detailed background. When I speak on leadership and innovation, I highlight other credentials. If it's a womens group or for entrepreneurs I showcase my books directed at that audience. It's inevitable as you increase in celebrity that you will speak to more than one of that type of audience, so re-purpose those bios and topics. Even if you are just doing podcasts, you want these ready to go.

In creating your bio, write in third person. For example, "Jane is an expert gemologist from Iceland who is the best selling author of The Definitive Guide on Diamonds", etc.

Create a folder on your desk top called MEDIA20.. (Current year and keep it updated)

In this file you will keep and name accordingly, with dates, so you know what needs updating:

BIO 200 (quick version - have it in both PDF and word)

BIO 400 (longer version)

Head-shot 1: Professional (include a high resolution for PRINT and a .png or .jpg file for web)

Head-shot 2: Your Style (label all shots FirstLastnameTitleDate.jpg etc.)

Don't have shots over 2-3 years old and update your photos if you change your look.

Speaker One Sheet: this is your "advertisement" as the expert/speaker. Include speaking topics, specific benefits to their audience, relevant quotes, testimonials, credibility points like your latest book or logos from organizations you've spoken to.

Why Hire Sheet: Top 8-12 reasons why company/association/et al. should hire you. Describe the results they and/or their audience can expect or what they get when they bring you on. Have this be all on a one or two page sheet congruent with your branding.

Top 10 Asked Questions: this makes your interviewer happy and their job easier. Think through what questions you want to answer to best showcase your expertise.

I would also have in this file your top articles on your branded stationary.

Try to get any TV, .mp4, radio spots, .mp3 or other press, but only if it's excellent!

If you have a demo reel, this is where you want to keep it. But you can also showcase the reel on your website, if it's excellent.

I would keep all of it in three places: one on your desktop, another copy on a thumb drive, and the third is optional; if you intend to do a lot of publicity, keep it on-line, either Dropbox or directly accessible from your website.

Then keep them updated and label each version so you know which is the current one instantly.

You've got this!

SEEK A SPOTLIGHT SOMETIMES

As a business owner you should be putting yourself in situations daily where you have an impromptu speaking encounter. So be prepared! It pays off.

First, let me take some pressure off though. If you follow the art of negotiation you won't ever feel uncomfortable about speaking again. Because the most important thing for you to do is - LISTEN.

Then, it's how you listen.

Don't listen with an edge or attitude, or waiting to get your turn in or rehearsing what you think you should be saying. Instead take a calm presence where you really concentrate on what they are saying. Look them in the eyes and really hear them. Breathe and wait for them to finish speaking. Then confirm what they said as to what you heard them say. Share back what you heard them say. "It sounds like you really like hiking adventures, had a rough experience, enjoyed your honeymoon..."

I took a powerful training in Non Violent Communication with Dr. Marshall Rosenberg. It's excellent in terms of handling any communication from business to personal. Sometimes people say things that can potentially land on us as hurtful, like a client complaining. I'm not a fan of complainers, but I do listen and appreciate feedback, as it's vital to the success of any business. And it will be for yours too. So listening from a calm place, while not taking on their comment as a personal attack, but understanding and acknowledging them and their deeper needs, is powerful.

Do this a few times. Then I want you to notice you didn't have to do very much "speaking" and you had ZERO impromptu words.

So you never have to be in your head again, worried about what to say. Just listen, you'll know what to do next. Even if it's just to say "WOW, I heard what you said. And, wow!"

SAYING NO

Saying NO means saying YES to what you really want. That's what happens when you get away from the confusion that feeds on itself in the world of entrepreneurs, service providers and coaching.

Each day, know who you are and what your key focus is. This will make it much easier to say NO when you need to say NO, because you've said a very loud YES to what you really want.

What is the number you need to reach today? How many outreaches, follow ups, proposals, etc? What must you get done that day? It may only be a 90 minute block of work and then the rest of the day you can loaf around. Fine. Just have that clarity.

Watch out for the addictive traps that are not restorative. I would set up a lifestyle that fosters your values rather than diminishes.

Learning is a core value for me, but not just for learning sake. I want to understand the why and how of things, and in doing so, I gain more overall wisdom. You probably read a lot like I do, but make sure you read for understanding and application, not just as a random action or to say you did it.

We all walk that fine balance of wanting to have all of the knowledge, but getting in the arena and taking action is what really matters.

CASE STUDY

I had a client who was one of over 100,000 graduates from a holistic nutrition school. She had popped up a website after graduating, hoping to get work.

When she came to me she was confused, frustrated and burned out. She had invested in a done for you, funnel/social media marketing program for $30K and between the fancy website, the cookie cutter funnels, the social media ads and other add on systems, she was near broke. With no significant results to speak of, she was raw, feeling broken and terrified of her future.

After our initial intake and assessment, I discovered she had already been a registered dietitian who had been working, unfulfilled and unrecognized, at a nursing home for years when she tried to do the on-line thing.

She wanted to transition to being a private health and nutrition coach so she could travel more. In building her framework, I asked about her personal passions, what inspired her, what uplifted her. I uncovered her passion and personal practice as a Pescatarian as a way of eating and she attributed it as healing her anxiety and depression.

Her eyes lit up when she talked about where to source clean, wild caught or healthy farmed fish and even on building a fishery in the Peace Corp.

Wow. Now we were uncovering her true dynamite. Her expertise was clearly on a specific way of eating. This was her thing. It was her lifestyle, and she knew it because she lived and breathed it.

She was unquestionably the expert in this lifestyle and she had a lot to say about it.

I continued to probe. What was she against? Well, she was adamant that vegan diets and latest fad diets were awful and spoke with authority against it. Another point of differentiation. Hmmmm. I was watching someone explode with clarity and confidence, credibility and power.

Listening to her, it was obvious! When I mirrored back what she said to me in the framework of clarity around her business, she nearly cried. What's more, after the initial, "can it really be that easy?", she literally shifted before my eyes into a confident, focused woman and a revitalized business owner.

Why make things so much harder for yourself? Can you see the simplicity of Model 4 Business and how practicing C4 Mastery unfolds? I sure hope so.

With her crystal clear clarity and renewed confidence, we took the next actions. Her key words were easy to find. The clientele who ate that way or were interested in learning more, tended to be lucrative, well educated people, often traveling the world. They would happily pay a premium for an expert. They were not, however, on social media platforms nor would they be responding to an ad through that format. They looked for their authority through their private doctors and peers, as well as a couple of premium magazines and specific podcasts. Now we knew where to target her marketing and PR efforts!

With a few more critical pieces in place, we shifted her copy and keywords, wrote target specific articles and created her media kit.

When she announced her new focus, she landed a client on the spot. She began getting noticed, referred, sought after and most importantly profitable.

While she had already been in a high priced coaching program, following 'signature system', niche finding, discovery call, funnel model that so many do, none of it made sense in her big picture.

But until there is clarity, we tend to look outside for the answers and often it's incongruent to you and your business. Rarely do the cookie cutter systems work as well as they are promoted.

Now that her clarity and confidence was in place around her expertise, she knew exactly who her clients were and how to communicate with and to them, no more guess work or random actions or tactics. She really didn't even need a website, and frankly most get this backwards. Often thinking if they have a website they have a business.

We did however, fix the copy on her site so she could still use it as a credibility piece and to house her media kit for speaking at, you guessed it, medical retreats on exotic islands where her ideal market attended and where her referrals came from! She even found a sponsor and was paid to fly to exotic ports of call, as the expert meal consultant for high powered executive retreats.

We had a bit more work to do on letting go of the old ideas (which weren't really old, they just didn't fit her). Once she cleared those, she was soaring across all areas. When the cookie cutter, copy cat facade started to fall away, before our very eyes there was a blossoming and the gorgeous light came back on from the inside out.

Since I record all of my sessions, she was able to go back and rekindle the moment of clarity and see within herself, how her confidence grew loudly and proudly, with each decisive step forward. This is a key piece I think we all must get in the habit of using. We can't brush off these micro wins. They are the building blocks of tremendous momentum in our C4 Mastery.

Within a couple of weeks she had her pricing and packaging (she now had 2 core offerings instead of unlimited) in place, simplified and tailored to her elite clientele. I suggested she meet with a couple of her past clients and reach out to the leading doctors in her area. In less than 90 days, she booked two top clients on a "dream assignment", up-leveling her personal life as well as generating more revenue in 12 weeks than she had in the previous 12 months.

The kind of C4 Mastery that unfolds when you practice Model 4 Business is almost like magic.

But you have to do the work.

Until you have that clarity, trying to force a niche or lock down your pricing and packaging, makes no sense at all. It's like trying to shoehorn an elephant into a Mazda Miata. Rough and messy. Sadly, so many still try to keep forcing it anyway.

CHOP WOOD, CARRY WATER

There are always going to be those people who have become addicted to looking for the next information product, coach or program. What's really happening is they are avoiding doing their right work at the right time, in the right way. I personally have hundreds of downloads, most of which I have never even opened. There will always be the next "hot trend", webinar or countless look alike, instant success programs or events, willing to take your money.

It is more important than ever to own your power and work on your C4 Mastery. Your attention is a very valuable commodity, if you don't protect it vigilantly, it will be stolen right out from under you.

Understand that the Internet and smart phones are powerful and wonderful tools for our businesses and to keep us connected. However, they are being used by every other business out there to try to get YOU to buy their product or service, even if you don't need or want it. If you are clear that you need it, by all means, invest. If not, don't.

Your solution is not another information product or another coaching program. Your solution will be getting to the right actions, at the right time in the right order. And they are the few, not the many. In fact, you will find yourself a lot less busy with far greater results, when you get practicing C4 Mastery.

Stephana Johnson   www.model4business.com

Remember, it is the day in, day out, moment by moment, correct, consistent and persistent actions that pay off in the short and long term.

It is the diligent pruning of the constant deluge. It is stopping the bleeding of the very addictive pattern of finding the next shiny object or copying someone else.

You know better now.

You will go to bed every night clear on what to do next and how to do it. Confident that you are taking right next actions that are in harmony. Each day you must begin again. As the old proverb says, 'chop wood, carry water', we too must get up and ignite the fire with purposeful passion.

Just as we have seasons of life, there are seasons of our business. Each morning, and throughout your day, align your energy to your definite major purpose, reviewing your objectives and what top 3 actions you will take today to move yourself toward your goal?

Some days you will be more focused on researching and developing, some days it might be connecting and follow up or networking and conversations. You will have your days where it is a focus of consistent delivery, correcting and improving your own skills, business or brand. Days of planning, promoting and sales. We will have the days where we need to be celebrating ourselves, our business and our clients. And so it goes.

Each day, back to the beginning. Ideally having expanded within the framework as a continuing upward spiral.

Always remember to create expansion, balanced and grounded in harmony with your values and framework. Don't worry about being stuck in a boring process, it's that stable foundation that allows for greater innovation! As entrepreneurs we must make room for the creative, visionary time, while also maintaining the mundane. Chop wood, carry water. That's how we get it done.

WHY I WROTE THIS BOOK

I wrote this book because to my knowledge there is no single book that lays out a clear, simple, proven, step by step, model for business for coaches, consultants, trainers, artists or others who offer a service.

There are excellent books on marketing, business, sales, PR, but none of them address the subject from this perspective. The reason I feel this is so important is because there are so many programs out there for people like you and me, that only add more confusion, self doubt, lost time and lost money.

Over the past 3 decades, I have not only actively participated in building successful businesses, I have observed, from and at, different levels of celebrity and success, and I have a perspective of the pitfalls and breakthroughs unlike anyone I have ever known or read about.

It is in my nature to share my knowledge and to support others. I also really like to simplify matters and get to the root cause of something. Many times I'd see peers go after the next fad and sign up for another coaching program promising miracles after it hit all surveyed pain points. I'd hear from colleagues who were scrapping their successful actions to start a podcast or launch a channel, because that's what the "gurus" were now doing. These can be workable tactics, if they are part of a clear strategy with determined metrics to measure results. But outside of that, they are a significant waste of time and incredible distraction from your goals and dreams. What's ironic, you don't even need a business card, a website or social media page to be successful.

FINAL THOUGHTS

I have thousands of books on my shelves, I have read more than half of them. They are tabbed, noted and highlighted. I have five bins of notes and dozens of 2" 3-ring binders full of notes and courses and programs I have invested in over the years. Not a single one led me to this moment.

My transformations came from two things: the right mentoring from the right person and getting clarity in alignment with my framework.

Confidence and credibility came from doing the right actions, in the right way, at the right time. Sometimes it meant getting up at 3am to write, or speak on a podcast on the other side of the world. Sometimes it meant taking a red eye to speak on a stage that put me in front of 25 of my ideal clients so I could be home for dinner with my children.

It was, and is, the moment by moment, day to day, right actions; consistently, persistently, diligently, carried out as aligned to the framework I have described. That is what took me from $0 to over 6 figures in less than 8 months when I opened my brick and mortar studio. It's what landed me the lead in an indie film. And blessed me to home birth and home-school my children. It's what helps me transform my clients lives and businesses. And it is what will take you from student to C4 Mastery.

It is not the fancy 5 and 6-figure pop group coaching programs, nor the clique premium 1:1 programs, nor a cultist religion, idols or donation of time, treasure and talent.

None of this will give you the clarity and confidence to know that you are the One.

It is not the live events across the country, sharing on stages or filler in an audience with thousands of other undifferentiated, copy cats, hoping for the quick fix with the magic answer to instantly make them be credible and take them to 'stardom'.

It isn't the expensive networking groups. Nor contact management programs or funnels or any of the myriad of other overly- marketed programs, gadget, gimmicks, latest and greatest fad strategies so prevalent today.

It **IS Being** who you are at your core and discovering that for yourself, maybe with the help of the right person, who is honest, forthright and competent. Who helps you connect with your goals, not out for their own agenda.

It is you being your own best client.

It is you eliminating everything non-essential to your goal and purpose.

When you start focusing with clarity, your confidence

will continue to grow, your credibility is then inevitable. And as you celebrate each milestone, small and large, you will notice your own unique and tangible vibe of celebrity status, because it will be authentically and intrinsically yours.

I have personally stopped doing all the mass event mania. Not as a participant and certainly not in my work as a coach. I prefer genuine connection and authentic communication. I see much faster and more profound results with my clients this way.

I have zero tolerance for the BS. Being totally tapped in to my own inner power, I know I can help others do the same. I know how to keep myself tuned and firing on all cylinders, in harmony. And I can duplicate that with every client willing to do the work.

Stephana Johnson   www.model4business.com

WALK IN YOUR OWN SHOES

No one can know what another has walked through until they've 'walked a moon in their shoes'. Promise me that from here on out, you will never compare yourself to another again.

Never subscribe to another coaches list to see what she is doing and try to copy it.

Never watch another's video or Instagram or like their profile or be a part of a FB group that you don't care about, only to see how he is doing it.

What works for one, will not always work for another.

What worked for her, may not work for you. And that's a good thing.

One other key point I want you to take away from here is that there are far too many others putting up a really nice front, meanwhile, they are broke financially, corrupt morally, sick and tired physically.

They are out of harmony in most areas of life, struggling to get through the day. But you'd never know it from their $20K website and photo-shopped pics, and social media selfies in front of a rent-a-rolls.

But I bet you can now see through all of that, right?

Nobody should have to go through all of that to discover a better way. And if you did already, you are not alone! I've had my fair share, both as a spectator and participant. And I've written a book about it, so hopefully others can skip that nonsense.

Just like it takes 40 weeks to make a human baby; and it really can't be rushed if all is to be well, businesses take time to build. Mastery takes even longer. However, I have observed hundreds of clients catapulted to success because they got the Clarity, Confidence, Credibility and Celebrity the right way, their way, with the right support!

I have been the lucky facilitator to witness those powerful transformations take place. While I can't help 100% of those out there, I can 100%, help those that come to me, ready for real support in this way.

My C4 Mastery Program is about the body, mind and business. After all these years, I have observed that one cannot separate any one of those components from the others. They must all be tuned for harmony in a holistic way.

Once a year I take on a small group of highly motivated entrepreneurs, leaders and creatives, who want this level of mentoring and Mastery. If you would like my support or feel my expertise could help you and your company, you can complete an application at www.c4mastery.com/applynow

Stephana Johnson   www.model4business.com

While I strive to give you a complete picture of the Model 4 Business in this book, there are many subtle nuances for each unique situation and individual. Each has a different past, with goals and dreams specific to them. But I have provided you with enough information to get started.

In my experience the transformation comes about through the right action, at the right time, combined with the right support.

I'd love to be that person for you.

Holding you in your highest good and best outcome.

Abundant Love and Light,

Stephana

"THAT YOU MAY KNOW THE SECRETS OF YOUR HEART, AND IN THAT KNOWLEDGE BECOME A FRAGMENT OF LIFE'S HEART."

KHALIL GIBRAN

ABOUT THE AUTHOR

Entrepreneur, speaker, advocate and author, Stephana Johnson energizes audiences worldwide through her unique insight and holistic perspective.

The experience, tools and techniques Stephana brings to each client engagement invite and inspire lasting transformation. Best of all, she makes it FUN, and as she guides each client to discover their soul's song, their confidence grows loud and proud with each decisive step forward.

She lives a holistic lifestyle, treading softly on our planet by choosing a life of sustainable simplicity, abundant joy and passionate purpose, with her two dynamic sons and their feisty cat GiGi, in the beautiful Pacific NW.

Her business websites include:

SPEAKING/COACHING: www.stephanajohnson.com
BOOK: www.model4business.com
ADVOCACY: www.findjoybeyondtrauma.com
SPEAKING: www.powerhouseleaders.com

For media appearances, please write to:

stephana@stephanajohnson.com

Acknowledgments

This could not have happened without Kelly Johnson. He was my friend first, then my husband, then father of our beautiful boys and now my former husband and co-founder of one of my ventures, Kluba Creative.

Without the light and the love of the two most amazing and beautiful humans I've ever known, Ryder Kane and Daxton Kohl, I doubt I would even be here to write these words. You are the wind beneath my wings. I love you beyond time, beyond space and beyond all words.

I must thank my dearest friend Moni Castaneda, our shared values for family, homeschooling, ancient wisdom and holistic wellness enriches my life greatly. Our collaboration has meant everything to me and I am grateful to have the sister I always dreamed of in her.

My dear friend Heather Dunnavan who keeps it real, makes me laugh, makes me cry and grounds me whenever I need. Our camping trips, our talks on the gazebo swing, our walks around your dream gardens are always balm to my soul.

To Sabrina Lamberson, a steadfast wife and mother, entrepreneur and constant inspiration to me. She is an exemplar of unconditional love and support to so many, and I am blessed to be one of them.

To my mentor Brian Johnson, my swim buddy Grey Geppert and my Optimize Family. It's an honor to be part of our group of committed Optimizers, who show up day after day, to master the best version of ourselves, in service to the world.

To my wonderful clients who bravely open their hearts to create their own unique and wonderful transformations. I am blessed to learn from each as they step into their highest version of themselves.

Lastly, I am deeply grateful to my Higher Self. It brings tears of joy to my eyes knowing I am blessed beyond measure for the inspiration and inner guidance which facilitates the perfect unfolding of my highest good and best outcome and for all those I am blessed to serve.

www.ingramcontent.com/pod-product-compliance
Lightning Source LLC
Chambersburg PA
CBHW060844220526
45466CB00003B/1240